Who's managing your life?

Rediscovering who we are through the decisions that we make

By:

Manny Hall

Table of Contents

Acknowledgements

I want to give a huge thank you to my Lord and Savior Jesus Christ who has given me life, chance after chance, and the ability to become all that He called me to be. With all that I am I am eternally grateful that you still love.

To my mother and father who have paved the way for me to not only write this book but persevere through some extremely difficult times in my life. I have the most amazing parents and I will forever show my gratitude and appreciation towards you. To my sisters and brother; I honor each of you for always putting up with your little brother and believing in every crazy dream and idea I ever had.

To my friends and church family that have believed in me and pushed me out of my comfort zone; showing me how to have the courage I needed to truly walk in purpose. I truly appreciate all the meetings, long conversations, and encouragement to make this project complete.

And lastly to my little princesses and prince; Savannah, Aliyah, and Andrew; your daddy loves you unconditionally. You guys are the reason I keep pushing and never give up. As your dad continues to reach for greatness, I ask that you continue to do the same.

INTRODUCTION

Many times we find ourselves upset, frustrated, and confused by our lack of proper management in our lives. We quickly blame other people for the mismanagement of our emotions, fears, doubts, dreams, and goals. The reality is that managing ourselves is of high importance and only our responsibility. This book will help you understand why taking a step back to look at who is managing your life is the first step in taking back your life. Within this book you will find individuals that struggle in the areas of managing their lives, finances, relationships, debt, emotions, friendships, and their future. Do you find yourself unable to handle the pressure of managing certain areas of your life? Do you feel that you don't have the knowledge or education to manage your own life successfully? We have all seen the frustrated co-worker that blames their boss for the pressure they experience throughout the day. The truth is, it's not the boss's fault this person is unhappy in their occupation, home-life, and other relationships that are affecting how they feel and perform at work. This person needs to learn how to manage themselves at work while their boss focuses on managing their work responsibilities.

We have also seen the parent that is at their breaking point over a child that is failing their classes at school, continues to get called to the principal's office, and can't seem to be respectful in their interactions with the rest of the world; most notably their parent(s). This parent also needs management skills. Learning not to blame yourself because of your child's failures, attitude, and misbehavior will give you a sense of freedom. The child's progress might be slow and the pain overwhelming, but managing your emotions, responses, and character with your child can make a big impact on their performance. A child will quickly watch and learn how their own parent(s) manages their emotions, frustrations, and how they make decisions. When a child sees you as an irresponsible manager they will find the need to protest your instructions because they don't line up with what they are seeing from your behavior. You will never be a perfect parent, but you can continue to try to be the best parent you can. The truth of the matter is that we all have areas in our lives where we can become better managers. While we all possess the ability to be free from the concerns of what others think of us, at times it can be difficult and seemingly impossible to dismantle ourselves from those opinions.

I have witnessed first-hand the damaging effects of not being in charge of myself. In the past I have been shaken up by allowing other people to control the way I thought about every area of my life; and consequently I became a "people pleaser" in order to win friends and gain approval. Living this type of life became even more challenging since I was becoming even more uncomfortable with who I really was; in actuality I had no idea who I really was supposed to be. I got upset when other people made decisions for me when it came to my finances, where I would go to school, what I would major in, where I would live, who I would date, and what my ultimate purpose in life was supposed to be. Instead of taking back control over my life I continued to live with the frustration without any sign of relief. Once I gradually grabbed a hold of this confused man I no longer knew, I realized that I desperately needed a change. Some individuals around me became upset at my sudden change in perspective -- mainly because these were the managers that I had assigned for various areas of my life and they were now unemployed. What I realized after learning how to manage my own life is that it is a lot easier for people to manage someone else's life because in doing so they never have to look at themselves.

We can all take full control of our lives, not live in fear, and experience the greatness we all know is inside of us. If you are not convinced that greatness is inside of you then continue reading; very shortly you will realize your worth. Make the choice today to start managing your life. Fire the managers who were originally assigned to certain areas of your life and hire yourself as the new manager in every area of your life. Through my experiences there were many hurts, pains, and failures I went through from allowing someone else to manage me. Unfortunately, no one is exempt from experiencing the pain associated with criticism, disloyalty, mistreatment, and abuse, but we can all learn from these experiences and manage the areas we do have control over. The price we pay for not managing our own lives can look different for each person but what remains the same is frustration. If you are ready to experience freedom from the slavery of being managed by other people, take the first step like I did and read on.

While there are many more areas of our lives I haven't mentioned that we need to take ownership over, the areas mentioned within this book were chosen because they seem to be the most important. Not everyone was equipped with the knowledge, resources, and emotional stability to go throughout life managing these key areas successfully. If you are like me, unfortunately you did not grow up with the proverbial silver spoon in your month, which in some respects has caused some apparent challenges in your life. If you did grow up with financial security, emotional stability, and the encouragement you needed to be successful, that is great, but you still need properly manage your life. If you did not grow up with a great hand of cards that doesn't mean that you are lacking something, it simply means that you have to take what you have and do the best you can with it. Based on some of the research that was collected for this study, an enormous amount of women that were surveyed indicated that it became easier for them to manage their own lives when they didn't have anyone they could depend on for advice. The majority of men that were surveyed explained that having a mother in their lives that provided guidance and direction was great, but their friends that did not have that support seemed to be able to manage their own lives more productively.

Who's managing your life? No one can honestly answer that question for you. It will take some deep introspection without the opinions of others to get to that realization. Being able to self-evaluate you can see what areas have helped you in your past and what areas have hurt you. Getting to a point where you are managing your own life is the ultimate goal; free from the judgments, negative opinions, and emotional harassment of others. Put this book down for a moment and look at yourself in the mirror. Ask yourself, "Am I really living the life that I want to live?" Your answer to that question will tell you a lot about your past decisions and how you got to this place. If you are frustrated with the life that you are living, it's not the time to beat yourself up, but it is time for you to remove the distractions, the hindrances, and all of negativity you are surrounded by. Taking the proper steps to enjoy your life will not always be easy, and for many of us it will take a lot of work. Be honest and transparent at least with yourself. You did not arrive at this place of mismanagement overnight so the process that it will take to come out of it will not be overnight either. I believe that today can be your day of transforming your life into something you have never experienced.

The future that you desire can be yours if you are willing to put in the work for it. I am not promising that all of your dreams will come true, but I am promising that if you are willing to take control of your life then you will begin to see some drastic changes for the better. There have been some people that have been managing your life without your permission simply because there was no one else that would fill that spot. When your family members, friends, and even enemies saw that you were not in charge of certain areas, they filled the position without an interview or the qualifications for the job. It's time to provide exit interviews for those individuals that have been in charge of your life and managing areas they were never hired for. For the managers you gave the position to, you have to get rid of them as well, because they are no longer needed. You owe it to yourself to take charge and become the man or woman you were destined to be. The majority of the time decisions are being made without your involvement, which later causes an extreme amount of aggravation.

No longer can you live the same way, expecting things to change without taking an active role in your life. There are dreams, goals, and aspirations that have never been met that you will never get to unless you get in charge. Looking back on your past will tell you a lot about yourself. Every part of your being deserves to have you active in it; there is no way to continue on without frustrating the dreams locked inside of you. Your money can change if you are willing to change. Your relationships can change if you are willing to change. The most important part of who you are can never be seen by the world without your help. If not today, tomorrow, or even next month, one day you will have to rise above your circumstances to experience what life is like as a manager of your own life. This book was not written to give you step-by-step instructions on how to manage your life, but it was written to show you the importance of managing your life. Your life has value and it needs your participation.

Chapter 1- Who's managing your mind?

A life spent making mistakes is not only more honorable, but more useful than a life spent doing nothing.

- George Bernard Shaw

Too many of us fight a battle with our minds and emotions and often lose because the courage and strength that we need have been dismantled by our efforts to please others. We fight against the opinions and perceptions that others have placed on us, seeking to find purpose inside of these individuals that have no idea who we really are. Managing your mind is not an easy task and to be a manager in any walk of life means you have to realize some very important things. First, at times you might not feel like managing and give that responsibility to someone else, second, your subordinates (in this case yourself) will not want to be managed and desire to do what is comfortable instead, and third, as a good manager will you constantly have to examine if your leadership style is effective or not.

Let's face it, laziness comes upon all of us from time to time and in some cases it might seem easier to relinquish the responsibility of monitoring our minds to someone else. The problem with giving this control to someone else is they will not no matter how hard they try, be able to properly play this role effectively. Managing your mind is your job, and no matter how much motivation and practical things you learn about it, the real test comes when contrary thoughts come in like a flood. Identifying what it is you should and should not be thinking about is of high importance. From the moment that you step out of bed to the time that you go to sleep, your mind is constantly racing and bombarded with various thoughts. There might honestly be thoughts of suicide because of the tumultuous dangers and storms you find yourself in. Suicide doesn't have to be a discussion in your mind. You do have a reason to live.

The world needs you to thrive so your contribution to it can change its landscape. I don't need to provide statistics on suicide around the world because whatever number I insert will be incorrect by the time this book is released and read by you. If you have ever considered taking your life or currently considering it, please realize you have purpose. Not only do you have purpose, there are people that need your voice to get through tough times. Your children need you, your nieces, nephews, and grandchildren need you; your wife or husband needs you, but most importantly; you need you. Life may be difficult right now, so I won't sell you a dream and say everything will be great tomorrow, next month, or next year. What I can guarantee is if you continue to push, and have a different perspective on your life, things will begin to get a little bit easier.

What are you thinking about?

When certain images come into your mind it is your responsibility to decide whether you will entertain that thought or dismiss it. In some instances if you do not dismiss the unwelcomed thought it will become a welcomed guest that is hard to get rid of. The same is true for good and positive thoughts; when they come allow them to stay awhile instead of moving on to the next thought. When you feel excitement, don't dismiss it and say that something negative is soon to come; labor on that thought. If you are thinking about your dreams and goals, stay right there in that state and think about them for a while.

Think about your plans for achieving that goal, what it will take, who can help you, what distractions you need to get rid of, how long it will take, and how you would feel once you achieved it. Your mind is a very powerful thing and using it to your advantage will often times get you much further ahead in life. Use your mind to be more effective for your life instead of being ineffective by not using it at all. The question we all need to ask ourselves is, "What am I thinking about?" Are your thoughts getting you further away from your goals? If you are constantly placing negative and unproductive images inside your mind, you will only get those same things in your life.

Someone once said, you get out of life what you put in it. The same is true with your mind. Are you thinking of your future and what you want to see in it? I am willing to bet that you know there are areas of your thought life that you need to change. You cannot be this great and awesome man/woman with the same thoughts you have of yourself. In many ways your thoughts run your life. If you are tired of seeing things remain constant in your finances, relationships, career, and confidence, start thinking differently. You cannot afford to neglect managing your mind.

Every part of success is wrapped up in your thinking. God has given all of us a unique opportunity to change the world with our special gifts and talents. You have to be a good steward over what you have been given. Many times we know how great and powerful we are but we never see it manifest because doubt and fear begin to tell us a totally different story. Doubt and fear can play some really horrible games with our minds. This is why we have to reject those thoughts that we don't want to think about. You have to tell doubt and fear that they are not welcome to reside in your mind. The confidence that you sometimes experience after being motivated, encouraged, and inspired by someone you have to hold on to that. Some people will attend a church service and feel inspired to change but a few days after they begin to think about their doubts and fears more than what they just received. If they reflect back to that motivation, they will remember not only how great they felt, but how special, unique, and gifted they really are. They would remember that in the midst of their pain, disappointment, confusion, insecurity, and discouragement they do have a purpose and reaching that purpose will take their participation.

We cannot for a moment believe that we will be able to reach our goals without our participation. Obtaining assistance from other people is great and definitely has its place, but your biggest support has to come from yourself. If you don't believe in you, it will always be very difficult for someone else to believe in you. The feelings that you have are real and should not be discarded, but your purpose has to be greater than your feelings. Most of us don't feel like working on our goals because of the hard work attached to it.

If you consider for a moment all those that have achieved great success in every industry they have all had to get past their feelings to reach their goals. Michael Jordan was cut from his high school basketball team and felt rejected and disappointed by this experience, but he made a decision not to allow that experience to shape his future. Thomas Edison in the process of all of inventions tried over 10,000 different ways to produce his results. When he was asked about all his failures he explained that he didn't view them as failures; he merely saw them as ways in which his method didn't work. Let's also consider the young man that has just graduated college and was promised by the society he lives in that he would receive a great job. Unfortunately, because of the tough economy in his country and the limited amount of jobs available he cannot find employment in his field. Yes, this young man is very disappointed, wants to give up, and consider other ways to obtain money to pay his bills. He feels like he has been betrayed by a country that he believed in. He has every reason to be upset and angry, especially since he has been trying to find employment for over a year now. This young man has found the secret though; called resilience. He finally makes a decision that if he cannot find a job in his chosen field that he is willing to take a job a fast food restaurant and at a retail store; both which are only part time jobs. These two part time jobs are enough to keep his bills paid. He will continue to seek other employment as well, while he goes back to school to obtain his Master's degree. There are much more dramatic stories that you have heard about and your story might be better or worse; what remains constant is the need to be driven.

The important thing to think about is the ability that Michael Jordan, Thomas Edison, and this young man all had to push past their feelings to reach towards their goals. Your pain can push you to greatness if you allow it to. I dare you to push past your feelings no matter what you are going through and take full control and authority over your mind right now. You might be tempted to look at your situation and how hard things are, but if you can peak into your future you will grasp a glimpse of hope. If nobody else believes in you, start to believe in yourself, and know without a shadow of a doubt that you are amazing, confident, and great. I believe you are great as well, and whatever you want to do you can be the best at it, regardless of where you have come from or where you are right now.

Does your attitude need to change?

Thinking positive thoughts will also help your attitude. Even though the U.S. economy is still not where it needs to be, people are out of work, stress and depression are becoming more constant in the lives of people all around the world, you still have the ability to change your perspective. Your attitude about your life can be a lot better than what it is. Your negativity is not helping yourself, your children, your relationships, or your career. Change your thoughts, and change your attitude; keep your attitude and you will keep thinking the exact same way. Put a smile on your face. No matter how hard your life is things can change if you begin to have a different perspective on your life.

There are some that have had it better than you and there are also some that have had it worse than you. Some of my readers are in countries that barely have sustainable drinking water, while others live in fear for their lives at every waking moment. There are others that are incarcerated and haven't seen their family in years, while others barely have enough food to feed their children. No matter what you are going through make up in your mind today that you will adopt a new way of thinking. I am not making light of your current situation, and I strongly believe you when you say how hard it is; but if the situation cannot change today you can at least change your attitude about the situation. In terms of that struggle, have you thought about every possible scenario for getting out of that rut? Have you sat down, wrote out some plans that could possibly work? Instead of giving up, I dare you to keep pushing. I dare you to take control of your mind even right now and tell depression, stress, sickness, and financial hardship that it will not change your perspective on your future. There is an inkling inside of you that has been saying that you're going to make it out of this storm; and you have to continue to believe that no matter how it looks on the outside.

This will be a new arena that you are entering if you have never managed certain areas of your life. Be cognizant of that reality and be patient with yourself; but do not allow the uncertainty or fear to stop you from pushing forward. You might get to a point where you don't feel like examining certain parts of your life. In business when a leader determines that there are certain areas of their leadership that need to be changed or realigned they have to make the changes quickly; because every moment counts. There are so many great things inside of you that need to be shared with the world; by mismanaging parts of your life you are not giving the world the best you. By allowing someone else to take charge, this will cost you precious moments where you could have been walking in your purpose. Instead of giving the permission over to others or the pain from your past, I would suggest that it's time to determine what areas you need to be changed. Your life is much more important than you might realize. We all have experienced some type of pain from relationships, jobs, disappointments, and goals, but that should never stop us from pressing forward. The question that we have to ask ourselves is who is really in charge of our lives? It might be a friend, a manager at work, a girlfriend/boyfriend, a family member, or it might be yourself, that is simply mismanaging your life.

Despite what you might have heard from those that try to manage your mind, you are not a failure, you don't need someone else's approval, and the greatness that is inside of you can be realized with or without their participation. Your mind holds some pretty powerful thoughts. If we can get to the point where we are properly managing our minds, most of the negativity around us will no longer affect us the same way. Think for a moment about the goals you want to achieve and now think about what is standing in your way. What if the thing that is truly standing in your way is not a lack of resources, a person, or your past, but only you? We all have a drive to succeed within us, a burning passion to be great in the thing that excites us the most. The problem is that we also have a capacity to be persuaded to think negatively about ourselves. You might agree or disagree, but whatever we put into our minds eventually influences our thoughts. To go a bit deeper, whatever you watch on television, whatever music you listen to, the conversations that you have, will eventually influence you to make the right or wrong decision in terms of moving towards your goals.

Dark days

The harsh reality is we all have to deal with some arduous changes within our lives that are often times thrown at us without proper planning or preparation. While we cannot change the fact that changes will come, we can have a consistent perspective that says no matter what comes my way, I will learn something from it. A large part of managing our minds is allowing other people to share their insight, wisdom, and instruction to us, but figuring out what we can and cannot use. We are not on an island by ourselves. Tom Hanks in the movie *Castaway* spent the majority of the movie trying to figure out how to adjust to his situation. His only form of communication was with a volleyball named Wilson, who soon became his best friend. Even though Wilson couldn't actually speak, Tom Hanks was able to encourage himself in the midst of adversity through Wilson. I'm not going to share the entire movie with you since you might not have seen it, but understand that he does experience some very uncomfortable, dark days, in which nobody else is there to help him. What do you do in your dark days? Have you had a history of giving up during tough times?

One thing I know to be true from experiences in my own life is that you are either coming out of a storm, you're in a storm, or you're headed into a storm, and that has remained constant. We don't have to be tortured by tough times that we go through. I have learned that when I allow a thought to enter my mind and remain there for an extended period of time, it usually takes form in some type of behavior. For example, there have been countless times when I awoke and said to myself "I do not want to go to work," "I don't like my job," "I don't want to look at my co-workers, etc." These thoughts usually manifest into a pretty rough day for me. I find myself yelling at other drivers on the road (as if they can hear me) because I'm running late, snapping at my co-workers, and becoming easily frustrated at various job duties because of my lack of enthusiasm to be at work. Now don't get me wrong; there is no magical formula for liking your job or the experience of driving to work, but you can get to a place where you are at least content. Let's face it, we might not enjoy the jobs we have but we always have two choices; quit or stop complaining about it.

There are decisions that we have to make through our minds on a daily basis; from the shirt you will put on today, to the gas station you will stop at to fill up your gas tank. These might seem like small decisions but they get a lot bigger and come with even greater risk if the wrong decision is made. Managing your mind takes a lot of courage and effort daily. Allowing someone else to do this for you has gotten you to the point you're at now. Taking full control of the decisions that we make will reduce some of the frustration that we all experience when others don't make the right choices for us. No other time in your life is it more important to take your God given right over your life.

You have goals and a vision that are extremely important to you and need to be realized. You cannot continue in the same crazy cycle of unrealistic expectations, pleasing others, and simply not enjoying your life. The individuals in charge of your life want to make every decision for you. They will either ask you a lot of questions regarding certain areas of your life so they can be better advised, or they will closely observe key areas of your life so they can become the expert for you. The problem is that you should be the expert, not someone else. The managers of your life want to bring you to where they think you should be; and if you don't honestly know where you need to be then the advice will seem extremely useful. Some of the suggestions your managers give are truly from a good heart, so use wisdom in accepting suggestions or discarding it if it doesn't fit into the plan you already have for your life. Some people specialize in managing other people's lives, but they cannot properly manage their own. It's interesting that some individuals will tell you how to manage your finances when their finances are out of control. They are consistently late on their own bills but they have suddenly become your financial counsel and have a great budgeting plan for you. These same individuals have a credit score that is too embarrassing to speak about, yet they have the confidence to provide credit advice to you. To be fair, it's not that a person that is struggling cannot provide great advice; the problem is not using that same advice they are freely sharing with you.

What if you enjoyed your life so much that you didn't need to take a vacation from it? What if you had so much control over your life that you were no longer entangled by the perceptions of other people and you lived; truly lived? What would you start or accomplish if you were not afraid? The unfortunate truth is that we are often times standing in our own way. Yes there are unforeseen obstacles, but if you can be totally honest with yourself, you have set yourself back. There might be other people managing your life but you still have the right and authority to make the right or wrong decisions. Instead of beating yourself up for some of your bad choices, why not start making good choices today?

We can't go backwards and correct our mistakes, but we can learn from them. John C. Maxwell wrote a book called *Failing Forward* in which he shared practical ways to bounce back from adversity and past failure. We all will fail from time to time but the question is when you do fail, will you learn from it and keep moving forward? Looking back on some of my past failures, I thought that I would never recover from, simply because I had the wrong perspective. I believed that making certain mistakes would shatter any hope of achieving my goals and aspirations. I believed that since I had already been given chance after chance and I continued to blow it, I would never be successful. Once I figured out how to learn from my failures and use them to my advantage my life suddenly changed. I saw that these mismanaged thoughts were hindering my growth in a lot of areas. Managing our lives is no easy task, especially when you have been used to mismanagement, no management, or the wrong management.

Criticism

Some people down right despise criticism because they think it is a demeaning approach to destroying their entire makeup. If taken constructively criticism can be a tremendous blessing since it sometimes carries much truth alongside it. Over time criticism has become one of the worse words in our dictionary, and the thought of someone being critical towards our behavior, perspective, or personality has pushed many of us to two extremes; "people-pleasing" or "aggressive rebellion." In a broader sense criticism is a person's honest assessment or evaluation of what they think about a particular subject or person. When someone gives us an evaluation that we agree with or seems to come across nice and pleasant, we normally don't consider that criticism, but words like: approval, appreciated, praise, or acceptance are easily received.

We all have the right to be appreciated, accepted, praised, and approved, but there is a time and a place for criticism in order for us to grow. Growth is a necessary precursor to reaching success in any area of one's life. If everyone around you is only telling you how great you are, you probably need to get some new friends, or at least some new associates. We need criticism. If your closest friends and family members only want to make you feel good about yourself and not tell you the honest truth, they are doing you an extreme dis-service. Criticism is also important in your business. If you are an executive that is not performing at the level expected of you, criticism might soon be knocking on your door, but don't shy away from it, embrace it. Take what you need from the assessment and move on. Examining yourself and allowing other people to provide their assessments might hurt if you are just coming to this realization about a particular issue that needs to be worked on. Would you rather have people in your life that will tell you exactly what you want to hear, that could be all lies to merely appease your ego? Or would you rather have someone that truly cares about you tell you the truth that hurts your ego, your confidence, or the man/woman you thought you were? Sometimes we think we are a lot greater than we are. When you are at the place where you cannot receive any correction from anyone that is a huge problem! Part of being great is identifying areas where you can be greater and working on them. You do not have super-human powers that disengage you from the rest of the world, and enables you to avoid dangers, hurts, and fears; you are only human. Since we are merely human, and will experience at some time or another the same feelings as the next man/woman.

If a trusted friend, family member, or advisor is brutally honest with you take that information they shared and see what you can do with it. I have a Pastor at my local church who is honest with all its members when they see him one-on-one. He doesn't sugarcoat anything because he realizes that we all have a job to do, and a purpose to work towards. I can appreciate my Pastor because he is more concerned with my future than my feelings. On many occasions he has told me things that were extremely difficult to receive at the time, but as days went by I not only accepted it, but I allowed the wisdom to transform my life.

You need to actually hear that the reason you got fired from that job is you were late too many times and didn't perform as well as you should have. The reason why that man/woman left you is because you refused to stop certain habits or you did not make them feel appreciated, valued, or supported; instead of saying they were not right for you. The reason why you didn't get approved for that house is because you have bad credit, are horrible with money, and there isn't a bank in the country that should trust you with a loan right now. The reason why your home got foreclosed is because you were not paying the mortgage on time, you spent more money on stupid expenses to keep up with other people, trying to impress them with things. The reason you can't find a good job is because of your lack of education and training. The truth has to be told in love and in a respectful way, but it definitely has to be told. Either you can tell yourself the truth, or hear it from someone else but the message needs to be heard, received, and acted upon quickly. This is all part of managing your mind, when you are able to receive tough criticism without allowing it to defeat you. When a person welcomes criticism they are able to obtain a new perspective and valuable insight, since not every person thinks the same way.

Refusing to manage any area of your life breeds frustration, anxiety, discontentment, regret, and a host of other feelings. At this point in your life you cannot afford not to manage your life. There are some areas in which you hear a desperate cry for management where you have made mistakes, forfeit your dreams, and caused relationships to fail due to mismanagement. In a sense you need to become a leader over your life in the same way that you have leaders over you in work, school, church, your city, state, and country. Another important reason to manage every area is to produce the confidence to stay in charge through each stage of your life. At times we can lose hope after experiencing some defeat in certain areas, and might feel we no longer have permission to stay in charge.

The life that you deserve you will never encounter if you don't take charge today.

While some people might not be extremely excited when they find out you are finally managing your life, you have to press forward. Some people that are connected to you cannot handle the success that is awaiting you in your future. Figuring out who should stay and who should remain is another large part of managing your life. At the same time, you also need to determine what habits and other activities are pushing you further away from your success. You cannot afford to stay surrounded by individuals that appear to be in our corner, but are holding onto ulterior motives. The unfortunate truth is that some people remain in your life simply because they feel empowered to manage someone else's life. Is it not interesting that the majority of individuals that desire to manage certain areas of your life have a more difficult time managing their own lives?

Managing your mind can be difficult at times especially with the anxiety attached to it. Thinking of that dream, that goal, that desire you are hoping to reach should provide the strength and passion you need in order to push forward. I realize how hard it is when there are so many other responsibilities you have in terms of children, your career, school, and relationships. You still cannot refuse to manage your mind will open the door for someone else to take that place for you. Taking it one day at a time is a good start. Find a notebook and a pen and begin writing down what is truly important to you, what things you can live without, and what areas have gotten out of control in your life. Only you really know what has been mismanaged in your life at its deepest level. There are some things that can be seen on the outside as a result of your mismanagement, but only you know what steps you took to get to this place.

As a people, it's a lot easier to blame other people for our bad situations and circumstances. It's not your family's fault, it's not your bosses' fault, it's not God's fault; we have to take responsibility. Yes, there were things that happened in your past that you had no control over happening to you, but with the hand that you were dealt it is now time to get up from your pity-party and make some decisions that will re-shape your future. Blaming others will never solve your problems. We have to guard ourselves from pride, which can tell us that everyone else is the problem, and we have no issues ourselves. Pride can slowly sneak upon us and steal the benefit that true self-reflection brings without its presence. Being able to quickly identify areas that you need to improve takes maturity and humility. Pride will tell you lies that will seem easy to believe since you are blinded by your own deception. When you get to the point where you desire to become better, the information that is rehearsed in your mind will be that of honesty even if it makes you uncomfortable. The focus that it takes to create a new habit starts with your mind despite the new, strange place that you find yourself in. Whatever you have planned for your life -- short term and long term goals -- you must determine how much they mean to you in order for them to be sustained and eventually realized.

Managing your mind will give you the needed strength to continue on in the midst of adversity. Every situation that we find ourselves in provides a learning experience. One of the reasons why we have so many individuals taking the position as managers in our lives is that they see a vacancy. You should be the most experienced person on how to manage yourself; not someone else. You have been equipped with everything you need to take control of your actions through your thoughts.

Chapter 2- Who's managing your finances?

This particular chapter will be very interesting, since most books on self-improvement either deal with finances or relationships. The reality is that managing your own finances can be one of the toughest things you ever have to do. Growing up is hard enough in terms of being responsible for yourself; getting up to go to work, handle daily important tasks, and paying bills. What most of us do not realize is that mismanagement or the lack of management of our finances causes so many more problems in other areas of our lives.

Who gives you advice about your finances? Do you feel you honestly have control over your finances? Our financial concerns, anxiety, and frustration often times come when we take the advice of other people and their plans end up not working for us. In this case, unfortunately, you cannot blame your close friends or relatives for making a bad decision for you. The bad financial decisions that were made which ended in frustration; were our decisions and nobody can be blamed. Managing your own finances goes way deeper than simply writing out a budget and balancing your checkbook, although those two things are extremely important. This type of management takes a look at the overall decisions you are making on a regular basis way before you make a purchase at the store; loan someone money, or pay a bill. Managing your finances the right way might be a daunting task for some people, considering the fact that everyone else around you is having the same struggle as well.

Credit and debt management

I have seen debt ruin the lives of many men and women; and what is even more frightening is the pain that it causes entire families. When individuals are not equipped with the right amount of knowledge of how to deal with their finances it can put a huge strain on relationships. If you are a man reading this book, it is time to "step it up" and be the most responsible person in your household; whether you are married or not. If you are married, show your wife and children by example how to handle money. Show them how to use credit responsibly and effectively. Sit down at least once a month with your spouse and go over your monthly budget, explaining your successes and failures financially.

Be the man that you were called to be even while you are single. As a single man you have a perfect opportunity to begin saving a little bit out of every paycheck to be prepared for when you do meet the woman of your dreams. Obtaining a ring for marriage or obtaining a house to live in won't be that difficult for you. This is a perfect opportunity for you to pay your car off, get out of debt, and start to pay your monthly bills three months ahead of time in the case of possible job loss or emergency. One of the most important things you can do during this time is to write down and accomplish some of your short-term goals. For those that are currently married or have been married you know how difficult it is to juggle going to college, raising kids, and attending to a spouse. With that being said, if you are single, try to obtain all the education you can while you are still single so your focus doesn't have to be divided. I know that I just spent time speaking directly to my male readers, but if you are a woman you can definitely apply some of the same things. You know there are things that you can change about your financial climate as a woman; do them now while you are still single. It doesn't matter how old you are; as woman you can be financially free; unencumbered by financial stress and worry. Your goal might not be to ever get married or re-married if you are divorced; but you still have to live so you might as well learn how to manage your money the right way.

The unfortunate truth is most adults were not told about money at a young age from their parents, grandparents, or other caregivers. Just think of the impact that schools could make on our society and in the lives of our young people if they educated them about money and credit. Many of the mistakes that I made early on after I became a legal adult in the U.S., was largely due to my ignorance in terms of money and credit. My first few weeks of college I was presented with the opportunity to apply for two different high-interest credit cards, which made me very excited at the time. They were attractive to me because they both had high-limits as well. I signed up with the cards and when they arrived I immediately used them. I purchased clothes and shoes and ruined my credit within the first months of having the cards. When the credit card companies begin calling asking for their money or at least a payment, I avoided them like the black plague and never responded. It literally took several years for me to understand money and credit and to finally get my credit intact. Most of our parents were also ill equipped with the proper knowledge of what debt is and how to manage money.

Debt in and of itself is not a bad thing; it can be used as a blessing in many ways if handled correctly. For instance, if you use a high limit credit card to create leverage to build up your credit score, or a personal loan to obtain a car or home, that is a good thing. Unfortunately, a lot of individuals use debt in a negative way, which ends up hurting them in the long run. Abusing credit and thinking that you are getting over on the system will only hurt your credibility down the road when you need it most. Maxing out all of your credit cards to purchase clothes, shoes, televisions and other items will only provide temporary satisfaction. Something that provides long lasting peace, joy, and fulfillment is saving money, having your bills paid on time, and having a decent -- if not great -- credit score.

Building up your credit with a diversity of credit cards and various loans can definitely help to improve your score.

Paying your bills on time might appear to be self-explanatory but this is one of the foundational aspects of sustaining good credit that a lot of people miss. Experiencing hardships with money can quickly lead to credit problems as well. Managing your money coincides with managing your credit, which should not be overlooked no matter how much money you currently make. Credit is used in all countries in some way, shape, or fashion. Its purpose is to provide you with the opportunity to receive a good or service before paying the full amount of its stated value. Some countries use credit more than others, and in terms of the American dilemma with credit I would say we use credit too much. Yes, we should definitely provide individuals the opportunity to experience some of the benefits of life such as driving a new car, buying a home, and shopping, but some people have abused this luxury.

To take it a step further, some people have abused their credit so much, while receiving the chance to file bankruptcy over and over; there is no question as to why our economy is the way that it is. Some people want to blame our economic condition on the stock market, others or corporate greed, and even political interferences; but I think it starts with each American being accountable to their own finances. I definitely believe that everyone deserves a fresh start when they get into financial troubles and experience hardships. If filing bankruptcy is the best option then that is understandable. The problem is most people are not managing their finances -- they are being ruled and controlled by what they want instead of what they need. You can be much more productive with your finances if you realized the power of money and your credit. One of the major problems some people have is spending too much money or things they don't need. Staying in your own lane with your finances will keep you from the dangers of overspending and allow you to stay within the confines of financial safety. There will be instances when you might want to take a risk, but knowing where you are financially and how much risk can be taken is a large part of managing your finances.

As a life coach I help a lot of my clients get a handle on their finances, and one of the most common issues is not having enough money to pay all of their bills at the end of each month. Another huge problem is they are in credit card debt and they see no way out. What I help my clients see is that no matter how far are, there is still an opportunity to be financially free. There are a number of different fears that are attached to money and credit problems; especially when you have been in that situation for so long.

Your struggles can turn into your success if you are able to learn from them.

If we spent more time focusing on what would make us money and instead of what will lose us money, we would put ourselves in position to make more money. Within this book we will speak largely about our future, goals, and aspirations. If you do have goals that you hope to achieve and money is needed to see them through, you might want to consider saving and/or building your credit. For most business ideas that you have, please understand that money will most likely be needed for the business to grow and be successful. You cannot neglect the importance of managing your money the right way if you want your future to change.

Things will remain the same and you will be no different from the family members and friends that are broke, struggling, and see no way out, if you continue down the same road. Your life doesn't have to remain the same. Identifying areas of your finances that need to change is only the first step. You then have to take immediate action to change those areas while the enthusiasm is still fresh. Most people that are broke, don't want to be broke, but they stay broke, because of their broke mentality. They do the things broke people do and neglect to follow the practices of the rich. The rich don't spend their money like the poor and broke do. There is big difference between the poor and the broke. The poor in some cases have arrived at that place without warning and it's not their fault. The broke have a similar story but the difference is they often choose to stay that way based on the behavior they exhibit. I would argue that in some cases we stay broke and desponded based on our consistent actions to spend our money unwisely, and in addition make horrible decisions with our credit and money.

Has anyone ever asked you to co-sign a vehicle for them? Have you done it? If you have ever experienced this process than you will know that 9 times out of 10 the individual for whom you are co-signing for will default on their loan and you will be stuck owing the remaining debt since your name is attached to it. Managing your finances is making wise decisions with your credit even if your decision doesn't make someone else happy. It's unfair for you to mess up your future to help someone else that doesn't care about theirs. If you take the time to investigate many of the financial problems that your friends and family have it is because of a lack of proper planning, budgeting, and carefree living.

In certain instances you should definitely try to help someone when you can, but if the person is not your spouse do not co-sign for any type of debt for them. This also includes children, who from time to time will find themselves in sticky situations and will ask you to co-sign for them a car or a house. You have to say no -- in a nice way or course. The practical implications for protecting your name is much more valuable when you put it into practice. It doesn't make sense to ruin your name for someone that doesn't care about theirs. The truth is, you won't be able to make everyone happy and they will not understand the path that you are on.

In many respects debt can seem like a ferocious lion seeking to devour anyone that comes into its path, especially those with a lack of knowledge and understanding to manage it. Debt can be a beautiful thing for individuals with the proper understanding of it. While some authors and talk show host advise people against having debt the reality is at some point in everyone's life having debt can actually help you. When we think of debt we have to shift our minds from the apparent bad debt and examine the other side of the coin, which is good debt.

Good debt can be credit cards, loans that you have used for leverage to start a business, school loans if they are used to further your education and eventually allow you to obtain a better salary, and even a car loan that is helping you build or to reestablish your credit. The majority of bad managers in terms of finances never want to review their credit report for fear that they will see something unpleasing to the eye. When was the last time you looked at your credit report? Looking at your credit report on a monthly basis might seem like a waste of time at first but it will definitely reduce the amount of added stress that could potentially come upon you later if this information is not reviewed. Go to www.creditchecktotal.com to order all three of your credit reports. The great thing about this website is that it gives you all three credit reports and scores for $1.00 for seven days. I would recommend that you actually pay the monthly fee of $39.95 because it helps you understand your credit, provides alerts if something changes to your credit, and gives you monthly updates of your credit report and score. Debt, if unmanaged can definitely cause a lot of trouble. The agony associated with ducking and dodging credit and collection agencies is not an enjoyable experience. Rather than running from it, it's time to address the issues surrounding your credit. There are plenty of helpful companies that can walk you through understanding credit and will help you become debt free. This chapter might be very challenging in terms of looking at how you spend your money, but taking the time to investigate your finances will save you some future pain.

What some people don't realize is being caught up with impressing others with materials items can quickly get them into major trouble. When a person doesn't pay their bills on time they usually have other areas of their life that are being mismanaged as well. Someone once said that instead of keeping up with the Joneses, bring them down to your level; it's cheaper that way. You can still experience the joys of material things but you have to be sure that your indulgences are not putting you in a tough position financially. I have known people that refused to pay their monthly bills on time, and instead pay for items they don't need. There are some people that want you to finance their needs while they take care of their wants. Managing your finances is probably one of the most important chapters of this book, and one of the biggest challenges that most people have. I would argue that the majority of problems that some people experience are centered on money and debt. Some say if they only made more money they would do better financially. In some instances their problem is not with the amount of money they make but what they do with the money that they do make. The amount of expenses you hold on a monthly basis can either hurt you or help you. If you currently do not make a lot of money one way to provide an immediate increase in pay is to reduce your amount of expenses each month. In addition, we all have to examine what we can live with and what we can live without. There are some that are reading this that make a considerable amount of money on an annual basis; if that's your story you should still examine your finances to see where you could improve.

Money

Considering things such as life insurance, a savings account, an IRA, mutual fund, a CD, or a 401(k) with your employer is definitely something to think about. It is never too early to begin planning for your future. Whether you are in college or getting ready to retire, it is extremely important to begin considering your future. If you haven't noticed already Social Security as we know it will not be available after the baby boomer generation, so every other generation has to be prepared. Individuals that are too concerned with their day-today living might not think about the importance of opening up a savings account or some type of retirement plan. Some people shy away from life insurance due to only being concerned with their own needs, but if you have family that you care about you should want to see them taken care of long after you are gone. There are some really great life insurance plans to be reviewed that can provide some assistance to your family members and friends after you are gone.

It doesn't matter what position you are in economically, your social status, or the degrees you might have obtained; financial struggles can happen to us all. The important thing to note is that you can be a good manager over your finances in spite of your situation. There are people that have had it worse than you but have done better, and people that have had it better than you but have done worse. You are much better than what you put up with regarding your finances. Many of us are tired of struggling financially but are not taking the necessary steps to change our outcome. Remember the definition of insanity: "doing the same thing expecting different results?" Fire the managers in your life that are in charge of your finances, department and take charge from this moment forward. You might need to write down some goals of where you would like to be in the next 3 mp give your family's name a better one than it currently has.

Let's look at Frank's management of his finances. Frank is a hard-working middle-age man that has done well for himself. He and his family live in a very expensive home in a suburban neighborhood. Frank has grown to be a great saver, great manager of his bills; and assuring that all of his bill are paid on time. He also invest into his company's 401k plan which has accumulated to such a nice portion that he and his wife will be able to retire without the stress of finances, but he has a problem saying no. Frank has a couple of managers in the form of his sister and two friends. His sister and two friends equally have control over Frank's finances in terms of giving. His sister always has an emergency where she needs to be bailed out of.

One time it was her basement that flooded so she needed to hire a company to water proof it, another time she had spent all her money on bills and needed help for the next few weeks, and lastly, Frank's all-time favorite; his sister was taking a trip to the Virgin Islands with her friends but did not have all the money for air-fare so she called her dearest brother for help. Frank's sister is one of the managers because she not only asks him for money, but she tells him how to invest the rest of his money that she feels he is wasting on bills. His two friends also provide some great financial management advice. They advise him that he needs to invest in their new business ideas every other year. The last few times Frank's wife tried to be supportive but after they had wasted thousands of dollars into business ideas that never turned a profit, she became fed up with Frank's friends' business ideas. His friends normally ask for money on a monthly basis since they are "entrepreneurs" and Frank should identify with the plight of a struggling entrepreneur. Frank provides as much money to his friends as possible for their businesses, cell phone bill payments, rent, or anything else that might come up. His sister and friends realize that Frank is going to take their advice and he is going to do what they say 95% of the time, unless his wife gets involved.

Does any part of this story sound familiar to you? Are you giving away money to friends and family that aren't contributing to their own financial progress? Maybe only a small portion of that story clicked with you; maybe your concern is not giving money away to friends and family, your concern is you don't give it to anyone; not even your bill collectors. This is an area of mismanagement that a lot of people find themselves in. Maybe your parents or guardian(s) never paid their bills on time so you never had a good example of it, or maybe you did have some good examples but you just have fallen into a bad cycle of not paying any of your bills on time. Are you managing your finances? The mismanagement of your finances is allowing your bill collectors and creditors to be the management of your finances. Instead of you paying your bills on time to avoid late payments and interest charges, you often pay the current bill a month later so in essence you are always behind. Yet some would argue that they really are struggling and it's hard to get out of the cycle without getting a payday loan which often times makes things worse. The same individuals that would hold that argument would have to examine the number of clothing purchases they make, the number of vacations they take throughout the year, the number of trips to fast-food restaurants, restaurant dining, and lastly the number of foolish purchases they make on various items because advertisements have manipulated them.

Again, there is nothing at all wrong with purchasing nice things, but if our goal is to become debt free and better with money, we have to be careful that we are not causing more problems on ourselves. We can't say that we don't have the money to pay our bills when we did have the money but chose to use our bill money on other things. We just have to use wisdom; if a financial decision will not help us in the long-run, it might be a good idea to reconsider. While there will always be advertisements everywhere we go; the reality is no one has control over you that much where you are forced to make a purchase that you did not want to make. Managing this aspect of your life would make you realize that you don't need to purchase something simply because an advertisement describes all its great benefits.

Many of us have seen at least one payday loan commercial on television, billboard advertisement, or road past one of their many buildings that are oftentimes positioned in lower-income neighborhoods. These payday loan establishments might appear to want to help but they end up costing you more money down the road due to their high interest rates on the initial loan that is taken out. While they offer you short-term relief for an emergency, you end up regretting the moment that you walked into their doors or applied for the loan on their website. Let's get back to the fact that these companies place themselves in lower-income neighborhoods. Have you ever asked yourself why are they placed in struggling neighborhoods? The answer is they know they can better capitalize on profits in lower-income neighborhoods because statistics prove that these areas have the most individuals that mismanage their finances.

Getting into the payday loan cycle can hurt you in so many ways. One reason it hurts you is that the interest rate is usually extremely high which causes you to end up paying much more back than you originally were loaned. And the other way it hurts you is that after taking care of a particular need/want you end up needing to take out another payday loan after you pay them back for the first one. There are some horror stories of individuals with three or four payday loans all out at the same time and they pay one back and take out a loan to pay another. The cycle is scary and never ending unless you refuse to pay them which in turn damages your credit score and report.

Let's now move into the entertainment part of your life where you go out with buddies, girlfriends, dates, parties, out with co-workers, and special events that you attend. Hanging out is not a bad thing to do; it usually takes some of the stress away as well as provides a time for laughter, memories, and plenty of Facebook and Instagram pictures. Unfortunately, this area has gotten out of hand for a lot of people.

Do you remember the last time you were unemployed and you promised yourself that as soon as you got a reliable job you would manage your money a lot better? During that time you did not have all the money you have now to spend on drinks, expensive dinning, and entry fees for a lot of the special events you attend. During that time everything was budgeted correctly; you knew for sure when you were in danger of spending your last $20.00. Trips to the grocery store were often accompanied with a list of some sorts, and all the purchases that you would have normally made foolishly did not get done because you were in survival mode. Now that you have this awesome job where you are making a decent wage, survival mode has been terminated and autopilot has been engaged.

Do you know why cars and planes have the option for cruise control and autopilot? It is because at whatever speed or altitude they are on or at they are comfortable with. Are your finances currently on autopilot or cruise control because you have gotten comfortable where you are financially and don't see a need to change it? What often happens in cars as well as planes are the unexpected dangers ahead. For a car it could mean another car suddenly stopping, which could cause a crash, or in the case of the plane, turbulence so strong that the plane can no longer remain on autopilot on this level; it now needs someone to manually control it. I believe it's time for you to take control.

Chapter 3- Who's managing your health?

This particular chapter on health might not be exactly what you expect to hear about your health. I hope to provide a more interesting perspective on your health in relation to who's managing it. We could spend a great deal of time talking about what to eat, what not to eat, and which diets are the most effective. I would like to argue that not every diet is for everyone and that too much of anything can cause harm to your body. I am not a nutritionist, dietitian, doctor, psychologist, psychiatrist, or even a counselor, but with my Master's degree in Organizational Management and currently working on completing my Doctorate degree of Education in Organizational Development I do have the experience and expertise of helping individuals manage their lives.

Your health should definitely be of utmost importance to you and while we all have a right to eat and drink whatever we want we do need to consider the long-term impact that certain foods and drinks have on our bodies. If your family has a history of high-blood pressure, diabetes, cancer of any type, or any type of rare diseases you have to take a stronger look at what you consume. While some people go with the notion that we will all die anyway; I don't believe that is truly God's best for you; and who wants to be laying in the hospital bed suffering because of the bad foods they ate over a long period of time?

Unfortunately, the average person in America doesn't enjoy drinking water so companies decided to create various substitutes and additives to make it easier for individuals to consume water. Another unfortunate truth is that a lot of these products, such as Crystal Light have as one of their main ingredients, aspartame. Aspartame is an artificial sweetener used as a sugar substitute in some foods and beverages. We have to be careful with this substitute because there have been studies to show that consuming too much of it over a period of time can cause the following symptoms: headache, dizziness, change in mood, vomiting or nausea, abdominal pain and cramps, change in vision, diarrhea, seizures/convulsions, memory loss, and fatigue.

Along with these symptoms, links to aspartame are made for fibromyalgia symptoms, spasms, shooting pains, numbness in your legs, cramps, tinnitus, joint pain, unexplainable depression, anxiety attacks, slurred speech, blurred vision, multiple sclerosis, systemic lupus, and various cancers. This information is not meant to scare you, but to make you more aware; and develop a desire to do your own research on the food that you are eating. Now in reality, some would argue too much of anything can cause problems to our bodies. Drinking regular water does some awesome things for your body and mind. Drinking soda does little to help improve any part of your body, and certain sodas can actually cause damage to various parts. If you are like some people, you might hate the taste of water and cringe at the very thought of drinking it, but you have to at least try various types, and if nothing else add some tasty fruits to make the experience a little less arduous. Who is really managing your health? If you are led astray by advertisements and marketing schemes then those companies are managing your health.

You have to take back control of your health and the decisions that you make towards it.

If you cannot take control then you will forever be told what to eat and what not to eat by other people, advertisements, and marketing schemes. When you walk into your favorite supermarket or retail store there are tons of advertisements that seem to call your name to purchase them. Some say it's never a good idea to go to the supermarket when you are hungry because you will end up buying more snacks then you intended; I find this to be true. The purpose of placing snacks in the front of the store and even close to the "check-out" lines is to awaken your desire to purchase snacks in addition to the primary reason you came into the store in the first place.

All snacks are not terrible for you, but the majority of them have a high amount of high fructose corn syrup in them. There is nothing wrong with enjoying a bag of chips, cookies, cakes, or pies, but the problem lies in the amount of these snacks that we enjoy. Most people would consider healthy snacks nasty, and something they could never even try. There are plenty of healthy snacks that are very good and not so much about an acquired taste as some might argue. The trick is trying several different products until you find something that you enjoy snacking on that is healthy. There are tons of healthy foods to consider; your health is worth the time and effort that it will take to find which ones you like. Aside from just the calories that you will have to burn, there are more chemicals than we have time to discuss in some of our favorite snacks in order for them to be preserved for a long period of time and taste so delicious.

Someone once did an experiment where there was a 24-count box of small bags of chips from a few years ago that had never been opened. The person conducting the experiment opened up several bags and found that all of them were just as fresh as a bag of chips that had just recently been purchased from a supermarket.

It's not just about you either; your family's health should be just as important. If you are anything like me, I have a hard time consuming certain vegetables because of the initial taste and texture. In order to get around this problem I purchased a nutria-bullet which allowed me to consume a good amount of vegetables and fruits each day without the hassle of sitting there eating them bite by bite. I have been using the nutria-bullet for a while now and I stand by it; it really works. Whether you use a Nutri-bullet, a smoothie machine, a juicer, or a regular blender, make sure that you are eating some fruits and vegetables on a daily basis. While some men and women hate to admit it, most men and women do not have enough bowl movements on a daily basis –sometimes waiting several days.

Someone once told me a funny joke about a man that had been experiencing stomach problems for several weeks off and on. He finally scheduled an appointment with his primary care doctor to see what was wrong. After several questions about his eating habits and trips to the bathroom the doctor concluded that he was full of crap. The man said, "What do you mean, that is highly unprofessional to say something like that?" The doctor said it again; "You are full of crap, you are not experiencing regular bowl movements; and your stomach is filled with too much waste and crap that needs to come out." That story always makes me laugh, but the cases of men and women that experience this is not funny at all. Drinking at least a half-gallon of water every day will definitely help you be more regular. Drinking tea is another way to get rid of toxins and waste within your body; but the most effective way is to consume a lot of water each day.

It starts at home

Aren't you tired of the endless cycle of eating better, working out, looking better, feeling better, being more confident, and then back to feeling horrible, looking worse, not working out, and eating terrible things all over again? Part of the reason that we continue to go through this cycle is that we get upset about things, are stressed out and/or depressed; and then feel compelled to indulge in our favorite snacks. I dare you to take control of your body and most importantly your mind in these circumstances. Have the courage to tell your body it will not take control of you and be pleased by everything it thinks it wants. You are in control, believe that right now, and stop thinking that you don't have control.

You are in charge, so act like it.

If you have identified some goals that you want to achieve for your body, then start today. The frustration will continue if you do not start living the life you know is best for you. As adults, we do what we want to do. When something is truly important to us we make it a top priority. We can make a million excuses as to why we are not working out and taking care of our body, but when we are finally tired of feeling horrible and not liking what we see, we will take action. Do you really want to grow older with the same body that you have now? Are you satisfied in private and you take all of your clothes off? Are there outfits in your closet that you cannot wear because you have gained too much weight? Are you embarrassed by the way your body looks when you are in public? Making life decisions regarding your body will keep you on this earth longer, and keep you from experiencing the pain and agony of common illnesses and diseases. Some people make the argument that they eat whatever they want because we will all die anyway. These same individuals end up in a hospital bed suffering through some painful surgeries to remove some type of ailment that bad eating or a lack of exercise has caused.

You might have been unhappy for a long time but you have not made the right decisions to take you where you need to be. Some people take advice from so many people regarding their health and wellness but never figure out what is truly best for them. You can watch a thousand infomercials, sign up with every fitness center in your city, subscribe to every fitness magazine, and have 10 different personal trainers; but still not be satisfied with your body. It all starts with you. Nobody can manage you, like you.

Many of us find ourselves going through constant physical pain, and in spite of what your doctor might have recommended to eat or stop eating you still choose to do whatever you want to do. Maybe the pain in your body hasn't affected you enough, maybe all the trips in and out of the hospital hasn't been enough for you yet, and maybe your slow demise hasn't hit home enough for you to start making some drastic changes. We live in a society where everything is quick and we develop a huge sense of impatience in every area of our lives. We don't want to waste time packing our lunch for work, so we go out for lunch, we don't want to deal with the long wait for our favorite restaurant so we order fast food, we don't want to deal with the agony of cooking a normal meal at home, so we buy quick processed foods that can be heated up in the microwave. Whether it is back pain, stomach pain, neck pain, leg pain, or foot pain; it all equates to a very uncomfortable consistent experience. I guess at some point you will get sick and tired of being sick and tired.

Your lack of energy and enthusiasm for your life is mostly attached to the pain you go through each day. Let's face it, it's hard to be excited about life when you know that you have to drag along a pain that refuses to leave. Your health problems can make a drastic turn with better eating habits and a commitment to working out. In many instances we feel that in order to become healthier we have to stick to the same regime as our neighbor or an ad we saw on television. The truth is creating and sticking to your own plan can eventually give you the results you are looking for. Also, keep in mind that just because someone is physically fit or has a smaller amount of weight, doesn't necessarily mean that they are healthy. Some people can eat a bunch of bad foods and still look great, but internally their body is suffering. There definitely needs to be a balance of the two. The main goal of managing your health is creating a realistic plan and not deviating from that. A diet in and of itself is only a temporary fix; but creating a lifestyle of health requires a change in many different areas of your life.

Preventative care is also extremely important for everyone to consider, having regular check-ups with your doctor can only help you steer clear of potential dangers. Unfortunately, there are some that cannot afford health insurance, but even more unfortunate are the cases with individuals with insurance that still do not schedule doctor appointments. If you have the means to see a doctor for regular check-ups, it is highly advisable that you do so. Just as important as your body is, your teeth are important as well. Regular dental check-ups for cleaning and examinations can only save you headaches down the road. While most adults are in love with candy and snacks just as much as children are, we have to consider the effects they are having not only on our body but our teeth as well.

Health professionals do their best to diagnose their patients when there are various symptoms that arise, but what is not done enough is preventive care. If our society as a whole promoted preventive care methods I believe there would be more healthy people and less sick people. Simple things like watching what we eat and working out a few times a week can help to improve our health drastically. Simply taking advice from other people is not enough since another person's plans and goals might not be the same as yours. For instance, if a friend is attending a gym and runs on the treadmill a few times a week and suggest that you do the same thing, this might not give you the results you are looking for. A workout plan including weights might be more appropriate for you.

Figuring out what is best for your body has to be done by you, not by someone else.

The reality is that with all the diseases and illnesses that are in the world we have to be extremely careful with not only what we consume but also interactions we have with other people. As I write this, the Ebola virus has killed over 4,000 people in Africa and one patient in the U.S. While this disease was not primarily in the U.S. the thoughts and fears of it spreading rapidly in the U.S. caused much fear. This disease had no mercy on the lives that it took -- leaving families torn apart and friends missing their loves ones dearly. Fortunately, there are other illnesses and diseases with cures and some can be prevented. We have to make the right decisions to take care of our bodies in spite of what the rest of the world is eating. I know that it is extremely hard when certain fast food commercials come on T.V., are on billboards, and other forms of advertisements, but your body should be more important to you then some temporary satisfaction. I am not saying that you should never eat fast food, that is your choice, but you do have to consider how it is affecting your body over a long period of time. Studies have shown the meat that certain fast food companies use are damaging to various parts of our body and a large consumption over a period of time can cause some forms of cancer. If you have children then you should definitely be concerned with the food that is brought into your home. Your children will watch what you eat and will follow suit.

Unfortunately, if you are used to consuming processed foods from the grocery store because it seems cheaper and easier to prepare, you are doing you and your children a disservice. You might be a stay-at-home wife/mom that has children to take care of or other household or business duties and it seems that you never have an adequate amount of time to prepare the kind of healthy means you would like to make, but you have to at least try; your family is too important. There are certain chemicals that are placed inside of processed foods that over a period of time can cause a lot of debilitating diseases; and if you are thinking of your children, its best to start now with changing some of meals you prepare for them.

If at all possible, try to purchase your food from a local farm or at least from a health food store like Mustard Seed, Trader Joes, Earthfare, or Whole Foods. There are probably a lot of other healthy grocery stores that you can go to that I am not familiar with, but give them a try. Many people think that it is too expensive to shop at some of these stores but in reality your health shouldn't have a price tag on it. If you are willing to spend hundreds of dollars a month on a car, purchase expensive clothing and shoes, and spend an outrageous amount of time and money at restaurants you have no excuses not to spend money on your health. If you are not in a position financially to purchase products at one of these stores, then at least try to eat more fruits and vegetables from the stores you go to.

Healthy relationships

We also have to keep in mind that certain relationships can be extremely toxic and bad for our health. If a particular relationship is causing stress, anxiety, depression, and making you doubt who you really are; it might be time to exit that relationship. Sometimes we can give people chance after chance due to the fear of loneliness and acceptance, but if that relationship is causing more bad then good, you have to at least evaluate it. These relationships that I speak of are not just with the opposite sex, it is with anyone; family, friend, co-worker, associate, etc. There should never be a situation where you have to put up with mental, physical, or verbal abuse. If you are married I am not saying that the only answer is divorce, but if the marriage is going to continue you should at least consider going to counseling.

Abuse can have a damaging effect on your health and cause some of the same symptoms as eating the wrong food for a number of years. Realizing your worth helps you to understand that there are some people that can no longer afford you. This is not an arrogant statement to make you appear better than the next person, but it is liberating in the fact that you understand that you are more valuable than you might imagine or comprehend. Realizing your worth reminds you that there are certain things you will not do because it goes against your value. Being free from constant arguments is a right we all have, and the entanglement that some people try to bring upon us cannot remain if we stay away from certain relationships. Relationships have the ability to hurt or help us; unfortunately connections to the wrong people can make our health suffer greatly.

This is not a proposal to remove every single person out of your life for you to be completely alone; that is not realistic. This reality should push you to examine or reexamine who is in your life, who should leave, and who should stay. The level of stress and drama attached to certain individuals is extremely toxic to your health. These relationships don't always have to be identified with a person you are romantically interested in, sometimes it can be parental relationship that is toxic, your child's mother/father, a co-worker, a friendship, or whatever else fits into this category. Only you really know what relationships are toxic and are affecting your health and well-being. Let's face it, some people are "Negative Nancies" or "Negative Nells", but their negativity should not be affecting you to the point of stress and anxiety. As I said before, it's okay to say "no" and it's also okay to stop texting and answering their phone calls. We've all been through some type of tough experience and need someone to vent to; but there is a thin line between venting and complaining. You honestly don't need that stress attached to you especially when you stop and think of all the heartache and pain you have been through. Think back to that last relationship you worked so hard to get out of. That relationship was literally killing you from the inside out. You barely survived with the peace of mind that you have right now. At times our relationship storms can be so daunting that we simply ask for a piece of peace. We want to live our lives but the relationship drains us to the point of exhaustion. We have permission to make our own decisions and live the life we want to live; free of regret and anxiety. Sometimes even though loneliness can seem like a monster to conquer, it is much better than being attached to drama. You have to come to an understanding that your peace of mine is worth more than the agony attached to companionship. I am not an advocate of grown adults staying single for the rest of their lives, but steering clear of potential problems or apparent problems I strongly agree with. People might try to convince us that we are crazy and out of our mind, but we know deep down inside that we're not crazy. Or are we? We have to take a hard look in the mirror and make sure the stress in our lives we are not bringing on ourselves. If you continue to date the same kind of man or woman and then complain about experiencing the same issues over and over again, then you are consciously or unconsciously placing yourself in the same situations. You can't cut your arm and blame the person next to you for letting you do it. Emotional health is much more important than we sometimes realize.

Mental and emotional health

Other than dealing with the food aspects of health we also have to consider our safety in terms of other activities that we engage in. We have to be careful of so-called fun activities that are dangerous to our bodies. I am not against being adventurous but certain outrageous behaviors that we take part in can are extremely risky and dangerous. You have to take charge of your health and still enjoy yourself.

Let's also take a quick look at drugs and alcohol. A lot of my readers might smoke cigarettes, take part in other drugs and/or drink various types of alcohol. You are a grown adult and have the choice of partaking in anything you want, but you have to realize that these things can also have an effect on your body in a negative way. You are a grown adult and this book is not intended to condemn you for your choices that you choose to make, but it is here to provoke certain questions that you need to at least consider as you go throughout your life. Can you the last time you saw someone that you went to high school or college with and their physical appearance made them look like they are a lot older than they really are? The reason for this is because after a period of time drugs, alcohol, and bad eating habits can wear on your body and make your skin look older than it really is. We all have seen or at least heard of stories of someone with lung cancer that continues to smoke anyway or the person diagnosed with diabetes that refuses to change their eating habits in spite of the physical pain they find themselves in. No matter what the particular illness or disease might be we still have to take care of our bodies. There are several different options out there to eat healthier and/or work out. Some things can be a slow process but other things need to be drastically changed depending on the results you are looking for. We only get one body and should take good care of it. The benefits of taking good care of yourself totally outweigh doing just enough or nothing at all. There is a way to have fun, enjoy friends/family but still be responsible with your body.

Our bodies were not designed to handle stress, anxiety, and depression over a long period of time. If you ever noticed when you are extremely stressed you will oftentimes get sick or become more susceptible to the flu. Your body should mean something to you; and making the decision of what to put inside of it will continue to be some of the most important decisions you will ever make. Whatever you need to do to decrease the amount of stress that you are experiencing, please try to make that adjustment as soon as possible. Many people don't realize this but simply watching a funny movie can release a lot of stress from your life. Stopping a text or phone conversation where the person is saying a bunch of negative stuff can help reduce stress as well. It's not that you should cut off all your negative friends, but you do need to set some realistic boundaries within that relationship so that it is not draining the life out of you. Some relationships do not benefit you at all and end up making you feel more and more depleted. Have you ever been in a relationship with someone that only focuses on their needs and wants but disregards your concerns? They want to share all of their stories, challenges, and issues but when it's your turn to talk all of a sudden they are too busy or have something else to do! Those types of relationships and/or interactions are not healthy and are a main cause of stress and anxiety.

In addition, if you deal with someone who is mentally, physically, emotionally, or financially abusing you, these relationships are on that same level of intensity. It might have surprised you to hear that you can be financially abused by someone. This simply means that you are dedicating your money and other resources to a particular person that is taking advantage of you and not offering anything back in return. They have put you in a bad financial position several times, promised to pay you back from money you have loaned to them, and continue to ask for more assistance. The individuals that have abused you mentally, physically, and emotionally have had a dramatic impact on your health, and if you can look back during those months or years you will see that your body was more prone to sickness during that time because your immune system had broken down.

There is a saying: "If you know better, you'll do better!" Unfortunately, we all know the benefits and consequences of what we eat but we continue to do whatever we want as if the consequences do not apply to us. I am passionate about this particular subject because I had a grandmother that died from cancer and spreading the word about the dangers of this cancer along with all the other forms is extremely important to me. Modern medicine seems to have advanced in certain areas but where I find fault is the awareness that doctors and nurses provide to their patients for preventive care. As medical professionals, their goal should not be to see as many patients as possible, but to limit the amount of patients that need to be seen so the doctors can focus on research. Doctors and nurses should be able to take care of those with serious medical issues and surgeries that are needed. One of my pain points is going into the doctor's office and being asked a billion questions as what brought me to his/her office. I am not saying that a doctor or nurse needs to be equipped with all the answers, but they certainly need to be more trained on educating their patients on preventive care techniques as well as a better approach to examining normal concerns that their patients experience.

There are definitely some great doctors and nurses across the world that work day in and day out to help their patients get well, but I wish that there were more medical professionals that focused on healthy eating. I also wish that there were more human beings that took a greater concern for their bodies and didn't wait until they were extremely to schedule a doctor's appointment. If you don't have a primary care doctor; do some research and get one as soon as possible. Sometimes we never know what's going on with our bodies until it is too late.

The same is true for mental disorders and disturbances. Counseling is just as important as someone going to the doctor because their heart or stomach has sharp pains. Having emotional health and stability doesn't just help you personally but it also helps everyone else around you. If you are single and planning to get married it is vitally important that you be emotionally healthy before getting married and really even before getting into a serious relationship with someone. Most singles want to rush into a relationship or even while taking their time only consider their financial stability, the safety of a home, and how well you can crack a joke with your potential partner. As you know there are so many other things that need to be considered before stepping out into a relationship. I would suggest that those seeking to get into a relationship or marriage go seek counseling from a Pastor, leader in a church, licensed counselor, or someone you respect enough that will evaluate your decisions with an objective point of view.

All of this ties together with your emotional health because if you are entering into a new relationship and you have old baggage it will make the relationship that much harder to remain successful. No relationship will be perfect, but do you honestly want to be involved with someone that has not dealt with the old man or woman that has hurt them; or a father or mother that walked away from them? The great thing is some people really work through their issues because they want to be healthy emotionally. They also realize that in order to have healthy interactions with others they need to be free from the pain from their past. We have to be open to help from others; we cannot figure out or handle everything on our own. Even though I am a Christian and I depend on God to help me through life I still look to people living on this earth to assist me in various areas. Dealing with our emotional health also has to deal with our relationship with our spouse, family members, and friends. If you have had a history of bad relationships with people and very short relationships you might need to consider how emotionally healthy you really are. If you constantly point the finger at other people, reject them, and walk away from relationships you might need to consider your emotional heath. Everybody else cannot always be blamed for the problems we experience in our lives. For many of us we do not understand how to work through certain issues so we sweep them under the rug and hope that they will eventually go away, but they don't. If you're married and your relationship is going great with your spouse, it's still a great idea to see a counselor just as you would receive an oil change or tune up for your vehicle – for preventative care. Your marriage should mean more to you than a vehicle and your emotional health for yourself and spouse should be a top priority. Don't wait until you start arguing and fighting, throwing things across the room and speaking badly about each other's parents to go get some counseling, get it before the problems start. If there are already problems be brave enough to get some help ASAP if your marriage really means something to you. In addition whatever other relationships that you have with people needs to be examined right now as well. The relationships you have with your parents, siblings, friends, and even co-workers need to have emotional stability so you are not frustrated and overwhelmed by being in a particular person's presence. As adults we shouldn't have to avoid anyone; figure out why you feel so much tension and stress attached to certain relationships. Even if the relationship isn't perfect you still have the right to have a healthy emotional relationship with everyone that you come in contact with. Get started today; managing your health.

Chapter 4- Who's managing your time?

Are you currently in a situation relationship where someone is stealing your time? Are you sometimes torn between taking care of your own responsibilities and saying no to someone that tries to make their priorities yours? Our time is one of our most precious commodities and often times overlooked and under-utilized. There will always be instances when you need to just sit on the coach to relax and do absolutely nothing, which can be extremely beneficial; but never become all out unproductive. Giving your body a chance to relax is a huge aspect of managing your time because without it you end up wasting time being burnt out or too exhausted to do anything. Don't ever confuse the need for relaxation with unproductivity, at times we lie to ourselves and say we are just relaxing when we know we are being unproductive. Our minds and bodies need an opportunity on a daily basis to recharge, since most of us are either going to a job each day, attending school, or raising a family. Giving yourself this time will also provide you with the opportunity to think, reflect, and conjure up ideas where you can become more effective in your daily task and in your future.

What are you doing with your free time? For some that have children to take care of on a consistent basis you might not feel like you have any free time; but when you do get a break, how are you using it? As I mentioned before there is nothing wrong with taking a step back to reflect, and as busy as you are this is healthy. You should consider what you can do to ultimately make things a bit easier for yourself and family. If there is a particular goal or aspiration that you have been pushing off because of a lack of time; instead of trying to block out several hours, take 15-30 minutes a day to work on that goal. For too long you have been putting yourself on hold for everyone else, but now it's time to revisit those dreams that have been tucked away.

Now it's time for you to confront yourself regarding all the time that has passed by without you making any real difference in the world. There is a reason why you wake up in the middle of the night, tossing and turning; your purpose is calling you. It's interesting, when you're great, average is not allowed in any part of your life. Have you ever noticed how frustrated you become at yourself and even others when an average performance is given in a particular task? Everything within you is screaming to live out your purpose. If you are someone that doesn't know your purpose, or cannot quickly identify your areas of strength, I implore you to read books that speak about purpose, but more importantly pray. Taking the time to pray can help reveal what your God-given purpose is, and helps you understand what is required for you to achieve certain goals. No matter what your childhood was like you have a reason to live; so act like it. Never let anyone how you back from experiencing the life you deserve to have.

Is time working for or against you?

Managing your time also means knowing when you need to regroup and refocus on what really matters. Since your family is important to you; no matter how big or how small you feel your purpose is; you need to live in it. There is an idea inside of you lying dormant that could change the world. You can actually get more time freed up if you take the time now to work on your vision and goals. This is not an attempt to persuade you to leave your job or drastically change careers, but it is an effort to push you to think outside of the proverbial box. You can experience life much more than you currently are. Currently, you are so busy in the usual daily activities that take up so much of your time; it leaves you little if any time to do anything you want. If you have children that you care for each day, I applaud you for working so hard each day. You guys are the real heroes. It's not easy being a full-time parent with all the responsibilities that are attached to your job.

For those that are in college or taking some form of training, it's best to study a little bit each day if feasible, to alleviate the stress of a huge project or assignment. I want to motivate and encourage you to push hard towards your purpose and don't give up merely because your reality seems antithetical in relation to your dreams. Your time is important; never forget that fact.

No matter what you want to do on this earth, time will either work for you or against you based on the decisions that you make. The small steps that we take towards reaching our goals end up getting us that much closer to what we are trying to achieve. One problem that we run into is thinking that time is so much on our side that it gives us a free pass to do whatever we want. If we waste our time, we never get that time back. It doesn't really matter what your ideas are and how creative you might be, we all get the same amount of hours in each day. There are some that go to bed early and wake up early enough to get a jump-start on their goals. It's unfortunate, but as Eric Thomas (motivational speaker) once said, "some people love sleep more than they want to be successful." I hope that is not you; sleep is great but you have too much work to do.

There is nothing at all wrong with getting sleep; I am a major advocate for sleep since without it you can't think clearly and be creative as you need to be. The problem that I do have with sleep is that it robs many people of the time they could use to work on their dreams. If your reality is not what you want then "tear reality apart" as Pablo Picasso once said. Instead of you conforming to the world, make the world conform to you. A great amount of men and women in our lifetime have been known as "change agents;" those who are catalysts for change. I believe there are also a great number of men and women that can be time agents as well -- those that use their time effectively to produce change. Now in terms of success I don't want anyone to go into the next chapter being ignorant towards my stance. I strongly believe that success is measured by your own personal definition, since what might be considered success for one person might be a complete failure to another. Reaching success for me is being at a state of peace, contentment, and satisfaction with the results that have been produced. In many respects I have reached success several times in certain areas, and in others I have merely had a glimpse. While reaching towards your goals and aspirations your time will definitely be your most valued possession. If you use your time wisely you will be surprised at how much extra time you have.

Time stealers

Unfortunately, there are individuals within our lives that desire to steal our time. To take it a step further, they not only want to steal our time but they want to abuse our time. The difference between the two is with stealing they might take minutes, hours, or even days out of your schedule to assists them with various things, but when they abuse your time, you end up assisting them with stuff that is not helpful to you or them. When a person abuses your time they devalue your time, they minimize the importance of your own tasks that need to be completed, and they misuse your time and mishandle it completely. You will find that some of the people that end up doing this the most are friends and family. If you really think about it, you wouldn't let someone that isn't that close to you have your precious time. It is a lot easier to say no to someone that you care little about than someone that you have given your heart to or you have allowed into your personal world. Even with those closest to us we still have to manage our own time properly; if we don't, then people will still find it necessary to take up our time for unnecessary things. Keep in mind that we still have an obligation to be there for our family members and friends, but not at the cost of misusing our time and not taking care of our own priorities.

I can remember times when a friend of mine would call me because they needed a ride to work and nobody else was available to take them. I agreed to take them to work in spite of the fact that I had a meeting scheduled around the same time they were scheduled to be at work. My plan was to be on time for this meeting, but I wasn't sure if I was going to make it, in light of my new responsibilities. I called the individual and explained that something had come up and I would be 30 minutes late for our meeting and asked if it were possible for us to reschedule for a later date. The person declined meeting at a later date and became very upset that I had to cancel our meeting at the last minute to take my family member to work. What I realized from that experience is someone else's emergency doesn't have to be mine, and just because I don't view your emergency as an emergency doesn't mean it's not;

it's just not mine. I also learned from that experience that some things are not a priority to some people until they get into a jam and then they realize how important something is. My friend knew ahead of time that they didn't have a ride to work and instead of being proactive they waited until the last minute to search for a ride. They called me because of my history in allowing other people to steal my time.

JUST SAY NO

There is an art to saying no. It is not rude, it is not mean, it is not inconsiderate; it is honest, frank, and freeing. When you adopt this art of saying no, you will no longer be held captive by what other people want you to do. At first it will seem challenging and the reactions you receive from those closest to you might make you want to revert back to your old ways, but you have to stay consistent. Saying no affords you the freedom to do what you want to do and think for yourself. Your time is important, even if nobody else believes that. I learned a long time ago that you teach people how to treat you, and if you are teaching people that it's okay to abuse your time, then they will continue to do so with or without your permission. When you say no you are telling the other party that you are able to make decisions for yourself and you are simply not interested in whatever they are suggesting at the moment. For example, if a friend is always asking you to go to the movies with her on Fridays but you just want to have a quiet evening at home alone, it's okay to say, "I am not interested in going to the movies tonight; I would rather just stay home." Now, keep in mind that your friend might not let you off that easy; she just might continue to ask you and give you every reason why you need to go to the movies. The reasons that she provides you with might be great reasons, but if you have made your mind up, just say no. Some of my readers in the U.S. might remember this; when I was a child there was a program called D.A.R.E. (Drug Abuse Resistance Education). I loved this program because the police officers that would come to speak to us explained that when we were peer-pressured to do drugs we were to "JUST SAY NO." That slogan stuck with me all of these years and when I am presented with offers, suggestions, and advice that does not compliment my destiny, I am reminded to "JUST SAY NO." In our personal and business affairs we have to be the same way: JUST SAY NO. Your life doesn't revolve around someone else and since your time is so valuable, if it's something you have no interest in, learn the art of saying no.

     I can recall times in my own life when I was productive in some ways but unproductive in other ways. I knew deep down that I wanted more for my life but the work that it would take to get there I wasn't ready to experience. In my early years of growing up as a leader at a church in Cleveland, OH, I had the passion and focus but I did not have the discipline, which showed up in my lack of character. There were many bad decisions that I made with money, my credit, with relationships, and especially my relationship with God. My pastor did an excellent job explaining what was expected of the leaders that attended his church, so in many respects I had no excuse. Instead of using my available time to read more books, study the bible, attend more conferences and seminars on business topics, and work on getting to know myself, I hung out with friends, and watched a ton of television and movies. During this time I had multiple relationships that I was in and out of where we sat around, went to various restaurants, movie theatres, and other events. As young adults we were focused on telling each other how much we loved each other and fantasying of what our lives would be like in the future. What is interesting is that every relationship I had during this time was with creative, smart, and brilliant women. I wasted a lot of time, not because I wasn't challenged but because I honestly didn't feel like putting in the necessary work.

I made up my mind that time was on my side and my early twenties should be spent enjoying myself. My pastor continued to emphasize how much potential I had and how great I would be if I stayed focused and used my God-given gifts to change the world. In 2003 I knew that it was time to start on my book, but it took me ten years to actually start writing it. There is no way for me to tell you that I didn't have enough time to write it or at least make some progress towards it in ten years. My pastor, through the years, had written three books, which made me tell myself, "There's more in you than what you're currently producing." It wasn't until 2009 that I got extremely focused and completed my course work to obtain my diploma in Theology; which provided the momentum to complete other goals. I then went on to obtain my Bachelor's degree in Organizational Management, my Master's degree in Organizational Management with a specialization in Project Management, my Project Management certification, my Six Sigma Green Belt (Process Improvement) certification, and as I write this book I am enrolled in my Doctorate of Education in Leadership development program. What I hope that you can see from my struggles is that time is extremely valuable. Being productive can catapult you into a different place of success, while being unproductive can make even the easiest goals seem troubling to achieve.

Who are you enabling?

I want to speak to another challenging area in terms of managing our time inside enabling others. Some people are just not interested in changing certain areas of their lives. This doesn't mean that you give up on them, but it does mean that you have to manage your time more appropriately so your time is being well spent. You know that friend, family member, or even co-worker that sucks up a lot of your time speaking about issues that you guys have spoken about a million times before. You want to be there for them, but each time you listen, provide advice, or help them get out of a crazy situation, they call you later because they are stuck right back in that same situation. I would dare to argue that in some cases they never truly got out of that situation from a mental aspect. At times someone can be geographically positioned in a new place but still have the same old mindset. This proves that though our locations sometimes change, if our mind doesn't we will end up repeating the same actions that brought us to a point of frustration. When you have individuals in your life that fit that equation, you have to set realistic boundaries that are appropriate for you. Part of the anguish that accompanies these relationships is their continual commitment to change that collides with their continual stagnation. Just as you have probably heard it said before, "If you can love someone from a distance, you can help him or her from a distance as well."

   To manage your time, you have to be a bit selfish to steer clear of those that will abuse your time without warrant. Enabling others doesn't actually help them, it hurts them. If you truly desire to see the best results and uninterrupted productivity from a family member or friend, it's time to let them learn some things the hard way. This doesn't mean that you totally forget about them or leave them stranded in tough situations; but you do examine the nature of their needs and decipher if they really need you or not. With the amount of things you need to accomplish that you have been putting off, do you really have time to enable someone else? Do you really have time to put your dreams and goals to the side to assist someone else that is not making their own dreams and goals a priority? You can want the best for someone and help them without wasting your time. I don't want you to think that I'm being harsh here; the only instance where our time is wasted is when we take part in things we know to be unfruitful and unproductive.

We should want to help others

I strongly believe that the world is waiting on you to come alive; the world is waiting on you to provide your creativity to assist with changing the world. There is no time like the present; which is often mismanaged in our attempt to enjoy every minute of our lives. Your creativity, regardless of which area of interest you have, is your gift to the world that nobody else can provide. You might have the same gifts and talents as another person but what remains different is your contribution with all the experiences you have had.

The frustrating part about not managing your time is that when you don't, someone else will see a vacancy in that management position. If your time was really important to you, then you would stop allowing people to waste it. When people see that you are unproductive with your time then will take an opportunity to step in and use that time for something that they feel can be productive. From the outside looking in it might appear that you are not doing anything with your life to some people, but if they really peaked inside a normal day for you they will see you are very productive. If they only knew that you work all day, come home and fix dinner, you're your children with homework, all without even sitting down for a minute to reflect on your own day. You then have to ask them how their day was in a caring and considerate tone, get them ready for bed, deal with the fact that they are not ready for bed, all the while trying not to break down, get upset, and lose your mind because of all the other responsibilities you have to deal with before your body tells you that it has had enough and shuts down.

The pressure and frustration that single parents and even married couples go through with children can never truly be explained; you would have to be a parent or guardian to understand. So again, at times people will look at your life and determine that you have some additional time to be a part of an organization, an effort to volunteer somewhere, a trip to the mall, a long exhaustive phone/text conversation, or any other thing that someone else feels you have time for; but you know that you don't. Your responsibilities are your responsibilities, and nobody is going to help you complete certain tasks but yourself. I don't know about you, but sometimes I would much rather have a phone conversation or an in-person conversation then a long-drawn out text conversation. The message can quickly get distorted and you are constantly wondering if you are misinterpreting what they are saying, or wondering if you're reading between the lines too much or too little. I am not against texting but in terms of our time, there are other ways to have a productive conversation. If you are handling a business interaction, text messaging is not the best method. I believe that texting is good for quick messages but in terms of a longer conversation, a phone or in-person conversation might be best.

It is extremely selfish for people to want your time and then abuse your time with meaningless conversations and activities that prove no value for your overall development and success. There is nothing wrong with having a conversation to laugh and speak on things that interest both parties, but when it is one-sided that is not fair. Have you ever had a friend that you were always there for but was never there for you when you needed them most? These are the situations that I am speaking about here; it's when you provide your precious time and give them undivided attention for a concern or issue that they are experiencing, but when you have a similar issue they are no-where to be found. If this illustration describes a relationship in your life, you need to examine the reasons why you are keeping this person around.

Mismanaging your time can be just as detrimental as someone abusing your time. You have goals that need to be achieved but you are wasting a lot of time focusing your attention on people and things that really should not be coming in front of your goals. In many ways, the thing that is holding you back the most, is you. You started this year with some realistic goals but based on your daily routines it doesn't look like you are getting any closer to completing them. Don't be the person that's misusing your own time, because when you have to look at yourself in the mirror and blame yourself, that is not a good feeling at all. Stop wasting your own time.

Removing distractions might allow you to have more time dedicated to what really matters. Your friends are important to you, I understand, but if they are really your friends they are not going anywhere. You need to become more productive ASAP with your time. You might have to miss a few dinners with friends, a few trips to the mall, a few conversations and other hangout events, but it will definitely pay off tremendously for you in the long run. We only get 24 hours within each day, so use it wisely. Your true friends will support your vision, goals, and dreams and push you towards them.

If you are in school and have weekly assignments to complete, why not knock those assignments out ahead of time and then go have fun with friends and family. If you are writing a book or working on the details for a business that you are trying to start, why not chip away at some of the important tasks and then go have fun. The main idea surrounding managing your time is realizing how important it really is. If you look back on previous experiences in your life, there have been plenty of occasions where you wasted money, but more importantly you wasted time. Have you ever watched a bad movie and thought to yourself that you will never get those two hours back? Have you ever been on the phone with someone and the conversation was so stale that you knew you had just wasted time but you couldn't get it back? We all have had experiences where we consciously or unconsciously wasted our own time. We will never be perfect but I hope that this chapter acts as a reminder that we need to properly manage our time.

Chapter 5-Who's managing your relationships?

Well-meaning friends, family, and co-workers all provide advice from time to time regarding your relational needs and desires. These relationships that will be mentioned are not just with a potential mate but deal with same sex friendships, opposite sex friendships, family relationships, co-worker relationships, and informal relationships. Before we really get into this chapter's discussion first ask yourself, "Am I a difficult person to get along with? Most of the relational struggles that we experience in terms of management is because we don't have an easy time getting along with others. Are you insecure? Do you sometimes wrestle with low-self-esteem? Do you like what you see when you look in the mirror? Do you have a hard time believing that you can be successful? Please answer these questions honestly; so you can truly get to the heart of the matter. Do you push people away when they try to get close to you?

It's not based on whether you are an introvert or an extrovert, it's simply that you push people away for whatever reason in relationships and find it easier to be alone. While you might interact with people on an everyday basis the reality is you keep most people on the outside of your life for fear that if someone got close enough they could potentially hurt you. The unfortunate truth is that someone one day will hurt you, but avoiding that potential hurt will also stop you from experiencing the joys of love and affection. The unfortunate truth is there are some very mean, rude, and inconsiderate people in this world; but everybody doesn't fall into that category. You might be missing out on some really awesome relationships if you continue to slam the door in everyone's face that approaches you.

Manage your own relationships

Everybody is not going to understand your mission. Some of your friends and family will tell you not to date, take your time, stay focused or simply be patient. While there is a time and season for those things, if you feel it is time and you know you are in a good place to consider dating someone then go for it. At times patience can be the enemy to progress. We have to use wisdom with our patience. Some people use patience as an excuse to remain stagnate. Again, there are times when we all need to remain still, but if you cannot show any type of progress in your life but you are hollering from the rooftops you have mastered patience; there is a problem.

At the same time if you want to remain single and focus on a career, school, your goals, a dream, there is nothing wrong with that either. Don't allow people to push you to remain single, and don't allow people to push you to get married; you know what is best for you. Don't be afraid to date; even if this person turns out not to be a good fit for you romantically, they could possibly turn out to be a great friend.

In addition, you might be able to learn a lot from that person and the experience of the interaction overall. That friendship could even turn into a business relationship, a close companion, or even someone you get awesome advice from time to time.

For those that are married, engaged or dating; don't search for something that seems better outside of your relationship with this person. Those that sneak around on their partner end up finding out that what they thought was better turns out to be a whole lot worse. These individuals might be lacking some vital things within their relationship so their hope is that someone else will provide these things. Cheating never solves the problem that initially drove someone to cheat. Identifying those areas of weakness within the relationship is a sign of maturity and willingness to make it work. If you want to give up on that relationship because that person cheated on you, then give up, but never make someone pay for their mistakes if you said you will forgive them. Understand that whatever punishment or consequences are owed to that person God will handle; that's not your job. You also don't want to stay in a situation where someone is clearly showing you that you are not their number one priority; and that they need others to fulfill areas of their lives that you cannot.

Relationships are difficult, let's face it. No matter how cute, handsome, or attractive someone is, at some point they will have to provide more substance to the relationship.

At times we put up with people without purpose and wonder why we are so frustrated. If you are pursuing your dreams and goals and someone is sitting around waiting on something magical to happen, you will not be comfortable in that relationship. It's not that your spouse, or dating partner has to reach for the same goals, but they do need to support the goals that you are going after. If it feels like a challenge for them to support you, they truly might be having a hard time supporting you. They might not believe in you, they might not think your dreams or ideas are good and worth going after. Bring this up in a discussion with them. Express your feelings regarding the lack of support that you feel within the relationship. If it turns out that the relationship needs counseling then get counseling, but if it's time to walk away; be brave enough to make that move.

You have the right to make decisions that are best for you; regardless of how upset or uncomfortable it makes someone else. If you know that your motives are pure in protecting your heart from relationships that could otherwise damage it; then do what is best for you. Too many times we stay in a relationship in an effort not to disappointment the other person. The truth is we will always disappointment or offend people from time to time. In some instances their expectations of us don't always match the expectations that we have for ourselves.

Keep in mind that not every relationship is bad for you, but some relationships aren't best for you. There is so much more for you to accomplish and if the person in your life is not supporting you towards achieving your goals, they might not be the one for you -- or at least not in this season of your life. You need someone that will be in your corner and act as your biggest support and cheerleader. There are enough people in this world that will provide negativity; but what is lacking is that push that will take you to the next level. Having someone by your side to believe in you and tell you how great you are even when you don't believe it yourself is extremely encouraging. One thing that is important to watch for is an individual that wants to use you. In some ways they might use you for money, but many times it can be for status, knowledge on a particular subject, motivation that you provide towards a dream or goal that they are pursuing, or a similar interest you both have. There is nothing wrong with helping someone but they relationship cannot be one-sided.

Valuing who you already have

If by chance, you have found a life partner that speaks life into you, loves, respects you, values you, supports you, and doesn't conflict with the purpose that is inside of you, then appreciate that. If someone is giving you all of those things that I just mentioned but you are not giving the same; you need to figure out why, and work to provide those same attributes towards them. It's not fair to give all of yourself to someone that is only willing to give you half of themselves in return. We need to value those in our lives that have shown a track record of dependability, commitment, loyalty, and dedication. We often times spend more energy trying to chase someone that doesn't want us or either hasn't shown their commitment to us. The ones that have always been there in good times and bad we should pay more attention to. When was the last time you simply called someone to say, "Thank you?" "Thank you for being there for me through that tough situation, thank you for allowing me to borrow that money when I didn't have any gas and my electricity was about to get shut off." "Thank you for praying for me when I thought that I was about to lose my mind." "Thank you for showing me that I do have value and potential."

We have to get to a place where we appreciate the faithful ones in our lives. We spend a lot of time dumping so much stuff on close friends and families but we seldom take the time to show them how much we appreciate their presence in our lives. Stop reading this book and text your close friends and family and say thank you. If you can't text them, then call them, if you can't call them, then write them, and if you can't write them then the next time you see them let them know how much they really mean to you. You have to communicate your feelings with all those you deem as important in your life. Some people think that communicating your feelings is soft and un-useful, but how on earth do you ever expect someone to know what is going on in your mind and in your heart if you don't tell them? Many times we assume that we know what someone else is going through or feeling; and end up being completely wrong.

Women especially have to take the time to learn and understand the men in their lives. Don't assume that his quietness means that he wants to be left alone; in many instances he might actually want to talk about what's going on but might not feel safe talking about it. Unfortunately, guys have been taught consciously and unconsciously since they were young that a man doesn't share their feelings or show any emotion so they grow up emulating what they were taught. Their fathers, grandfathers, and uncles always portrayed this "tough guy" image, which they watched closely. When these men in their lives felt any kind of emotions they stuffed them under the rug, and dealt with the pain in some unhealthy manner; such as drinking, smoking, anger, abuse, or some other unsuitable behavior. The few men they actually saw show emotion, or deal with pain in a healthy manner, were considered too feminine. If you care for that man regardless of the relationship status, take the time to hear his heart. This is a large part of managing your relationships.

Sarah's Example

Let's peak into Sarah's life in terms of managing her relationships. Sarah hates taking advice from co-workers and friends about her relationships with the opposite sex since most of the advice she receives never ends up benefiting her. She is not overly concerned with getting married any time soon but the thought of having a nice guy to go on dates with and have stimulating conversations with intrigues her very much. Yes, Sarah has been caught up in watching romantic movies and often reads romantic novels. The managers of Sarah's relationships often tell her that she is being too picky and that she needs to give some men a chance that she wouldn't normally be attracted to.

While this advice might not seem too bad initially, Sarah doesn't really know what she wants in a relationship and what type of man she would really be interested in. Taking the advice from her friends and co-workers seems easier for her since she doesn't have to take the time to figure out the values she expects in someone she would date. Yet again Sarah is not interested in marrying anytime soon, but she does want to date. On a few occasions Sarah's friend Emily set her up with a guy she knew from Facebook and expected them to hit it off as soon as they met. Emily had no idea that her Facebook friends' photos and statuses never told the true story of who they really were outside of social media. What Sarah quickly found out was that Roger's personality was outgoing and friendly on Facebook but in person he was quiet, passive, and extremely shy. It's not that these are bad qualities, but definitely not what Sarah wanted. When she explained to her friends how her dating life was going which ended in them giving her a long pep talk about giving Roger a chance. Sarah is eventually convinced to continue going on dates with him and even allows him to come by her house for various dinner dates.

Sarah's frustration begins to boil more and more and she doesn't know what to do. She asks her co-worker what he thinks and he explains that she shouldn't listen to her friends and stop contacting Roger immediately. Now Sarah has become even more confused. Her co-worker Cameron gives her other instructions, which were to go hang out at social gatherings and the first nice guy she sees she should flirt with to get his attention. Sarah tries going to social gatherings and flirting with guys, but it seems out of her comfort zone; to Sarah, something seems wrong about this approach. She goes back to Cameron to explain that she didn't meet any guys using the "flirting approach" and how uncomfortable it made her. Cameron tells her she will never find someone to date if she isn't willing to flirt a little bit with a guy. Sarah's people-pleasing addiction kicks back in so she goes against her own will and begins flirting again with various guys at socials gatherings. Still, Sarah becomes more frustrated. Sarah's frustration could have been ended a long time ago if she would have taken charge of her own dating life.

There might be some similarities to Sarah's story for you and then again there might not. The important thing to gleam from Sarah's mismanagement is that she was not in control of her dating life; which caused her friends and co-worker to step in for her. Taking advice from others is not a bad thing, but we have to gain a clear understanding of what we want and do not want in terms of dating; and stand by that.

Parental Relationships

Relationships do not have to be as difficult as we sometimes make them. From parenting relationships to friendships, to dating relationships at times we can complicate things. Some of the difficultly is not knowing what you really want from each relationship in your life. If your parents are still alive and if you are blessed enough to still have your grandparents around, you have to figure out what role they will play in your life and what role you don't need them to be involved in. At times we allow our parents and grandparents to influence so many decisions in our lives simply because we believe they have more wisdom in certain areas and out of respect we take their advice. They might have wisdom and great advice to provide you with, but does that mean that you solely depend on their opinion or do you take the time to really figure out what you want to do? Some of us have really important decisions to make and it might seem easier to take someone else's advice so you can look back and blame them for the bad decision that was made. In actuality they were not the ones that made the decision, you did! Our parents might mean well, but the areas that you are in charge of managing you cannot give them over to someone else to manage.

Due to the level of care and support that most of our parents provided to us, it becomes easy to not only listen to their advice, but also take it and give them the position of manager of your relationships. Unfortunately, there are some that are reading this book that have lost their parent(s) to death and others still have their parents alive, but they are disinterested in participating in their lives in any capacity. It is important if you still have your parents or guardians that you visit them, appreciate the role that they played in your life, and be there for them the best that you can. They might not have been the best parent(s) in the world, but in many ways they did the best that they could.

Unfortunately, many of our parents were not given a hand-book on how to parent; so they learned by making mistakes. Some of those mistakes caused you a lot of pain as a child and placed a strain on your respect that you have for them even to this day. I'm asking you to try your best to forgive them and understand what life was like for them during that time. I'm not making excuses for them, but I am trying to get you to understand that parenting is never an easy job no matter what the external conditions are. Some individuals work hard at achieving a goal or dream that a parent had for them before passing away. While that might seem like a worthy aspiration to fulfill some of the goals they had for you, if any of these things conflict with your ultimate purpose and responsibilities then you need to consider if this is counter-productive. In addition, there might be a negative opinion that a parent(s) had regarding some relationships you were involved in that is influencing certain decisions you now make. Just because your parent might not agree with you dating within a particular race, a certain type of person, being friends with a certain group of people, or you being involved in a particular religion, that doesn't mean that you have to listen to them. Evaluating what you really want is the most important thing. Managing your relationships gives you the freedom to choose who will stay in your life and who will not; based on what you say, not your parents.

The pain of relationships

The pain that is associated with relationships can sometimes be devastating. We oftentimes fall out with family members, friends, co-workers, and those whom we are dating for various reasons. No matter what has happened in the past I would like to remind you that there is more life ahead for you.

Although the pain is hard to get past, you owe it to yourself to work through the difficulty and manage this area of your life. Un-forgiveness can be monster to get past, especially if you have to deal with the person that caused you the pain on a consistent basis. The person that caused you the pain back then and is hurting you right now as well as long as you harbor un-forgiveness. I am not saying that you need to rush to forgive anyone, but what I am saying is you need to at least start the process. Dealing with painful memories of a past relationship can be very difficult and the reality is for most people revisiting those thoughts only makes them even more upset. Part of managing your relationships is figuring out what works and what doesn't for your life.

You might be in a relationship where you have expressed the need for someone to change over and over again but you are not getting anywhere. You might have made several attempts to communicate with this person but it didn't get you anywhere. Don't lose heart; even if you have communicated your concerns to your partner but they still are not changing; give it some time; seek counseling, and most of all pray. Keep in mind that if there is constant abuse within the relationship you definitely want to seek counseling and maybe even separate from that person for a season or indefinitely.

There are certain things and people that we put up with that we really should not. Instead of blaming the person that hurt you for every part of the pain let's look at what role we had to play in the demise of the relationship. As easy as it is to think of ourselves as angels, we're not; we all have strange ways about ourselves that make it difficult for other people to deal with us sometimes. Having a clear understanding of where you personally went wrong in the relationship can help you not to repeat the same mistakes within the same relationship or with another person in a similar context.

In addition, it's important that we understand what we can and cannot handle from every person within our lives. At times we attempt to handle things in certain relationships that we wouldn't in other relationships. For instance, if you have made it clear to some people in your life that being considerate, caring, and supportive is important to you then that should become the standard across the board for everyone to follow. What we tend to do is give some people a break from our standards and become upset when they go against them. If you set precedence early on in a relationship that you want to be treated a certain way and you don't receive that, than its time to evaluate what role if any that person will have in your life.

Someone once said, "We teach people how to treat us." While teaching grief recovery classes a few years ago (which is a small group support system that helps individuals get past any type of grief in their lives) I would often give them an example of someone stepping on your foot. If someone accidently steps on your foot you might look at them and wait for them to apologize for stepping on your foot. Whether you get an apology or not, you will most likely let it go and move forward with your life. But what if the person does it again, and again, and again? You will look at them the second and third time and probably say, "Excuse me," or "You stepped on my foot." Now if this happens a fourth and fifth time you will probably remove your foot from their reach so you don't have to experience the discomfort of having your foot stepped on again. You will also most likely be somewhat irritated at the person for continuing to make the same mistake at your expense. All in all, you had countless chances to let the person know it wasn't acceptable to continue stepping on your foot.

This example is similar to how we deal with pain in relationships. If someone does something against our wishes early on in a relationship we assume that they realize what they did was wrong and will correct their actions since they know better. When they continue to do the same thing over and over we still assume that they know better and will change their actions eventually. Unfortunately, time passes and it becomes a few weeks, and few months, and even a few years and the pain associated with that one particular action continues to hurt because the action continues over and over. At this point you become extremely upset and a conversation about that issue will probably turn into an argument because over the course of time your frustration has built up. If you would have addressed the situation early on if might not have gotten to this point. We often lose great friendships and potential dating relationships because of our past pain that is not properly dealt with. We can never assume that someone else understands how we feel on the inside if we never express it to them. Having unrealistic expectations within any relationship is dangerous, and will eventually hurt you in some way, shape, or fashion.

Managing this area of your life successfully will save you a lot of frustration. Nobody has control over you except you. You are in charge of your own life and are responsible for what you do with it. Too many times in our lives we allow other people to take charge and manipulate us into doing stuff that doesn't fit into our own plans. They force us into believing that the purpose they have chosen for us is more appealing than the purpose we know and believe we are to go after. You have to get to the place where your dreams and goals mean something to you. No longer can you walk around aimlessly through life never experiencing your best, holding onto the safety and shelter of other people.

We all need each other in various ways, but when needing someone stops you from living, that is a problem. There are those in our lives that expect an exorbitant amount of commitment and loyalty but they only give back an infinitesimal amount back to us. Are you tired of one-sided relationships where you are giving more than you are getting? Are you tired of being used for what you bring to the table but the table is clear and empty when you need something back? Instead of getting upset at the other person; reshape the relationship from what it is right now. Re-teach that individual how to treat you; stop putting up with the same discouraging words and actions from them. Make up in your mind that you are the most important person in that relationship. That statement isn't selfish; it simply indicates and confirms that self-preservation is the first law of nature. If you are not taking care of yourself you will never be able to help anyone else. If you allow other people to be your main priority all the time, you will eventually run dry on the energy to take care of yourself. Relationships should always be give and take, no matter who you are in the relationship with. There will be times when you give more than you are getting, but if you look at the relationship overall and you are always getting the short-end of the stick; you might need to evaluate the longevity of the relationship.

I would argue that the majority of the conflicts that we have with some of our close relationships is that we never truly realize who is managing our lives. We find ourselves wondering how we got to this point without considering the fact that someone else has always bailed us out of tough circumstances. All the various decisions we have made in our past have made us into the men and women we are today. Regardless of how good or bad those decisions have been, they were all your decisions. There have been some occasions when you were helpless and were not given the opportunity to make a choice, but I am speaking about the instances where you did have a choice. Taking back control of your life doesn't mean that you no longer accept advice or suggestions; it simply means that when a decision is made you are taking full responsibility for it and not blaming someone else.

It's funny, when we make a bad decision someone gave us advice for we blame them, when we make a good decision we usually want to take all the credit. Now this doesn't mean that you should never take advice from anyone else, it simply means that you need to review their opinions up against what your values are and the eventual purpose you are shooting for. There lies another common problem that arises in many of us; we do not have a defined purpose so we are walking around aimlessly. It becomes even easier for you to take advice from others and not manage your own life if you don't realize what your purpose is. Do you know your purpose; what you were really meant to do in your life, or are you just taking up space? The goal is for you to have a well-balanced life where you are in charge, but also welcome suggestions. Just as I mentioned earlier with criticism, we need to welcome it because whether it is true or not that is what is being perceived by your actions or overall demeanor.

My own relationships were run by my past hurts and failures. I thought that if I could just prove to the world that I could have a successful relationship with the opposite sex that I would be in everyone's good graces. Unfortunately, life did not go that way for me, nor does it go that same way for the majority of people reading this book. I had failed relationships in which I did learn a lot from but that in no way took away the pain associated with the launch and eventual crash of relationship after relationship. In addition, I left some wounded victims that wanted the relationship to go on but in my state of mismanagement, the relationships were bound to be unsuccessful. Figuring out what I wanted within a dating relationship was often blinded by fears of things going wrong, or the fact that so many others had hurt me in my past; I asked myself why would this be any different? Taking over this area of my life took a lot of strength and courage.

I wanted to be free to experience a relationship I heard was realistic. My past had run my life and convinced me that I was not worthy of a successful relationship that could turn into marriage. History told me that there weren't too many successful marriages in my family, and I wouldn't have one either. Society told me marriage was not that important and living a single life in which I enjoyed with many different women was acceptable by their standards. Getting to the point where I finally dismissed all of the thoughts that took precedence over my relationships, I began to understand why I was so unsuccessful in this area. By not truly knowing yourself or understanding what you like, desire, or are purposed to be, you run the risk of entering stages of your life that you weren't meant to be a part of. At times due to mismanagement we hook up with people that do not fit our destiny. Taking it a step further we marry individuals that do not complement our God given talents, gifts, and plans. Some of the frustration comes when we expect that person to live up to dream, goal, or aspiration that you have for them but they do not have for themselves. Out of loneliness and the fear of being single for the rest of our lives we agree to enter relationships that have early signs of disaster.

Keep in mind that it's not that the individuals you dated weren't great people; they just weren't great for you. We can ruin someone else's life by forcing a relationship that wasn't meant to be only to fill a void in our lives. That's almost as dangerous as eating a meal you know you are allergic to simply to satisfy your hunger. At this juncture, l completely understand that most people don't want to be alone. At the same time aren't you tired of mismanaged relationships that take up your time, resources, and energy?

When you are dating someone you shouldn't have to play games. You should feel free to be yourself and do what makes you feel comfortable. You shouldn't have to worry if you text or call that person too much, if you have went on too many dates, or what you should and should not say. We should always use wisdom in our communication but we should also feel free enough to be completely honest with them and yourself. If at any time you are concerned about too many text messages or phone calls, then bring it up to that person and have a discussion about it. Throughout the communication with this person you will get a vibe, discernment, and/or a sign if the relationship is going anywhere or not. Again, be honest enough with yourself and if it's not working or going anywhere, walk away.

If you are a considerate person and you feel someone is being inconsiderate then address it with that person, instead of being frustrated and harboring ill feelings towards them. There are certain things that are "deal breakers" for you when dating someone; make sure those are clear and concise with the person you are interested in. You also don't want to lead anyone on that you know you are no longer interested in. The reality is sometimes we like someone in the beginning of dating, but something has made us disinterested in that person and that is okay, just make sure that they know the relationship isn't going anywhere. What some people do is just stop texting or calling the other person hoping that they will figure out that they are no longer interested. As grown men and women we should have enough respect for ourselves and the other person to simply be honest about where we think the relationship is headed.

In addition, make sure that you are not posting messages on social media about them; speaking indirectly to them. I have seen individuals that were upset with each other create posts speaking to someone that hurt or made them upset and they make it known on social media without saying that person's name. The reality is relationships will hurt us, but if you cannot speak directly to that person by phone, text, or in person then leave it alone. Don't use social media to let out your frustration. The same applies to anyone else in your life that will potentially upset you and you feel you want to vent. This behavior of sharing your venting experience on social media never works the way you want it to. There are plenty of other ways that you can share how you feel without the social media world experiencing your frustrations.

Managing your relationships also means that you set clear boundaries not only with the opposite sex; though we have placed a lot of emphasis here, but every other relationship as well. Making the decision of how much time and energy is spent on each relationship is a huge step in managing this area of your life. If we are honest with ourselves, everybody doesn't deserve the same amount of time with us. Whether you are thinking about your mom/dad that you enjoy spending long hours on the phone with, or the co-worker that you insist to take lunch with them every day, you have to consider how much time you will dedicate to each relationship. It could also be the friend that always seems to have a problem or story you have to listen to, or even the person at the gym that wants to have a conversation with you while you're in the middle of a workout. There will always be people in our lives that need our support in some type of way, but setting clear boundaries within the relationship will mitigate some of the frustration that we experience. We all have dealt with the constant complainer that seems to suck the life out of you. This person by nature isn't always considered a negative person (though they can be); but they still greatly decrease the amount of energy you have after certain conversations with them. The danger with this relationship is the person is asking you unconsciously to manage areas of their life. They complain to you because they are hoping that you will continue to provide answers to their problems and if nothing else give them permission to remain stagnate. The complainer views you as their manager who gives direction and guidance; unfortunately they are often insubordinate if you ever suggest them to look in the mirror. We are all responsible for managing our own lives and everyone else is responsible for managing their own. Who's managing your relationships?

Chapter 6-Who's managing your mouth?

We have been told from the time that we were children to watch what we say, and that advice from whatever the source was needed. I have personally seen how not managing my mouth can hurt me in many different ways. I absolutely hate some of the things that come out of my mouth, and the timing of some of the words are even worse. Now when I say that I hate the words I'm not saying that there are swear words that are coming out of my mouth, but more the negative words and perceptions I sometimes have of myself as well as others. Being positive definitely starts with your mind, but even if a negative thought is there we have enough time not to speak it. We don't have to speak every negative thought about ourselves, a situation, or another person.

There will always be some things we go through that are difficult but we can learn to have a different perspective on the situation. Our mouths have the ability to set the atmosphere in our lives and even determine what type of day we will have. It's the classic example of someone waking up to an irritating alarm clock and getting out of the bed and accidently stumping their toe on the bed post. Immediately the person has a decision to think whether to be positive or negative. He/she can say out of their mouth "this is going to be a bad day;" which will set the mood and atmosphere for how things will be. This isn't some magic formula that if you say the right words you will automatically have a good day. I'm neither implying that difficulties will automatically remove themselves by you saying the right words, but it will keep you in the mindset of positive thinking which can definitely help your day to get better.

What are you talking about?

Communication is extremely important in all of our relationships, and neglecting this truth often leads us into arguments with those closest to us. We have to be mindful of the way that we speak to those around us. Spouting off rude words doesn't help to build solid communication. Some people will end up shutting down if they have experienced too many uncomfortable conversations with you. Managing our mouths is one of the key areas we all need to work on and have developed if we will reach our goals and achieve our dreams. The easy thing to do is to not communicate with anyone to avoid disagreements, but the mature thing to do is to manage your mouth properly. There will be times when you need to speak your mind on a particular issue with a friend, family member, or even a co-worker; but managing your mouth the right way gives you the wisdom to know when and when not to speak.

At times frustration gets the best of us and we end up regretting the words that so quickly come our mouths without thinking. We often say phrases like "he made me mad," or "she pushed my buttons." That very well might have been the case, but we have to control our mouths since we do not have control over someone else's. Instead of always venting to the person that actually hurt you, try writing down your feelings instead in a journal. For most men this is a foreign concept that a lot of women have been doing for years; but it is truly effective. Try grabbing a notebook or a journal and keep the dates, times, and your geographical location on each page that you write. This will not only give you a chance to let the feelings out in a safe, secure manner, but it will also give you the opportunity to go back weeks, months, or even years later to reflect back on those times to identify your progress with dealing with certain issues.

Another thing that can help you begin speaking the right words, is hearing the right words. Read more books that will not only encourage you to be better, but also provide a different perspective on your life, and in relation to others. Reading also helps to expand your vocabulary. For those that read the Bible, spend more time in it to reaffirm what you already know that can help you through troubled times. Not managing my mouth has gotten me into a lot of trouble in the past when I had nothing but negativity around me. It became hard for me to encourage myself when I didn't have anything to draw from within. Everyone around me reaffirmed how hard things were and all of us remained hopeless. Be careful when you have so much negativity around you that you begin to believe those things. If you constantly see everyone broke around you and hear all their sad stories about how hard it is and it's everyone else's fault; this will become your reality. You have to eventually disconnect yourself from those people and those words so you can get around positive people that are speaking positive words. Most of us love watching the news, but let's face it, there aren't too many good stories that are shared so the majority of the stories you hear are based on bad news. We already talked about the conversations that we have with other people and how hearing consistent negativity will eventually cause you to become negative in some ways.

You have the ability to make things change in your life by the words that you say. Start to speak life into yourself even if nobody else does. Tell yourself how great you are and that you have meaning in this world. You have been placed here for a reason and it's time that you start believing that. Don't allow the words that you speak to keep you from experiencing God's best for your life. Other people might have their own opinions and perceptions of you, but you do not have to agree with them. You can make the decision to see yourself in a different way; despite the past mistakes that you have made. You cannot always count on someone else to believe in you; waiting on their approval will leave you exhausted. I have a confession; there was time when I was a people pleaser, until I realized that pleasing people still doesn't please them. I had to decide a long time ago who would be managing my life and especially my mouth. It seemed easier to believe what other people thought about me and so I reaffirmed their perceptions by not only believing their thoughts but actually speaking them out of my mouth. During these days I would adopt the dreams someone else had for me and the thoughts no longer merely existed, but they received life when I spoke them. These dreams were not my own, and often times they did not even fit into what I knew I was purposed to do. So why did I believe these dreams could become mine? I assumed that someone else knew what was best for me so I allowed him or her to manage my mouth through the words that I spoke.

It's time to be quiet

Another large aspect of managing your mouth is not sharing your dreams with everyone. Just because you have received insight about a passion you have or a goal you will reach towards doesn't mean that you have to share it with the world. The right people will show up in your life for the beginning stages of a vision you have or a goal that you are reaching towards. Some people are tired of hearing about all of your big dreams and goals you're trying to achieve. The negative perceptions some people have of your dreams will continue to discourage you, if you keep telling them about them. The reality is, there are some that do not believe in you and they never will. They would rather you stay at your job for the rest of your life and never shoot for anything else.

At times, people will have more faith in your vision than you have. They might encourage you to go after those dreams simply because they see how your success will one day benefit them. Managing your mouth is so extremely important to getting to your next level and achieving the success that your heart yearns for. Everybody cannot handle what you have to say. Everyone is not equipped to receive the words that come out of your mouth. When you speak you have the potential to push people to their next level; the problem is some people around you are not ready to go where you are headed. This doesn't mean that they are bad people, it just means you might have to shut your mouth about certain things.

Sometimes you have to manage your ears as well and not listen to the negative talk from other people. The voices that you hear from negative people can sometimes discourage you to the point that you no longer believe in your God-given talents and gifts. You have to manage your ears in such a way that you refuse to call or receive text messages from individuals that are speaking death instead of life into you. In this season especially you have to work hard to purge yourself from negativity so that stuff doesn't carry over into your future. Since we cannot stop other people from talking about us, let's at least manage what we say about ourselves. The words that we say to ourselves are more powerful than anything that anyone else has to say about us. Believe that you are an amazing person regardless of who they believe you are.

Your mouth has the ability to help you or hurt you. Since we speak to ourselves the majority of the time, we have to think on things that are positive or that will at least encourage us to where we are trying to go. A lot of us talk ourselves out of achieving success by the negative words that we present to ourselves. Long before you ever heard someone say you can't reach that goal, or that dream is too big for you; you convinced yourself that it wasn't possible; and it only became easier to believe that lie when someone else confirmed it for you. What kind of thoughts are you thinking? What kind of words are you speaking to yourself?

Dream bigger, stop placing limitations on yourself. It doesn't matter where you came from or who you are right now. I would argue that we all have an opportunity to be successful if we are willing to work for it. That dream that you have is not too big, your goals are not unattainable. You can be successful. I dare you to expand your mind to believe once again, to hope once again. Dream as if you were a kid again and you actually had the faith that all of your wishes would come true.

About ten years ago while I was still in my early twenties I started doing something that changed my life. I was reading, "Think and Grow Rich" by Napoleon Hill. He spoke about the unconscious mind and how much power it has over our actions. Within the book he suggested writing down your goals and plans and a clear, concise way; placing it somewhere in your house, desk at work, or any other place that you frequently go. He advised to make sure you at least had these statements somewhere inside your home to see every single day. Next, he advised to repeat this statement you had written down several times through the day; but at least in the morning before you went to work, and at night before you went to be. He thought it was important for this to be the first thing we saw when we awoke, and the last things we saw before we retired for sleep. The purpose for this was to remind a person of their goals, plans, and aspirations. He believed that if you consistently did this and believed it would happen, you would be that much closer to achieving them. Hill argued that those things would eventually manifest because your unconscious mind would align all that was necessary in your path for your eventual success.

I strongly believe this to be true. The only exception I would make, is if your goals are not part of your purpose it won't bring you the peace and serenity that you are looking for. The main thing is to speak positive thoughts to the person that matters the most -- you. Any worthy aspiration that you have cannot be met with unproductive thoughts and bad words that you are sharing with yourself. When I say bad words I am not speaking about swear words or any other type of profanity. Bad words are the words that are not good for you to think about or speak; they are antithetical in relation to your dreams. If you are tired of certain areas of your life, change your thoughts and words. Again, this is not a magical formula but it does provide a solid foundation and a road map if you want to reach a place of satisfaction. You owe it to yourself to have a different future than your past has been. Some of you reading this book have experienced a great past and present, but there are others of us that have been reaching towards a certain goal or dream as long as we can remember.

Regardless of how someone else has done you in the past, you have an obligation to treat them with respect, loyalty, and kindness. Now this loyalty doesn't mean that you have to remain in their presence or allow them to disrespect you, but you remain loyal to them by keeping your mouth closed from speaking negative words about them. Managing your mouth shows a sign of maturity, strong character, and integrity. You don't have to say mean words to someone that has hurt you in order to be free from the pain they caused; you can be free by accepting what happened, dealing with the pain, and eventually moving forward.

In my past I wanted to argue with people, prove to them how bad they were for hurting me, and tell my sad story to the world. Unfortunately, the world didn't really care, even if it acted like it did sometimes. My mouth got me in all sorts of trouble; especially when I also wasn't managing my emotions. I would say a bunch of mean comments and hurtful words back to someone simply because I felt I needed to defend myself. A true statement once said, "Hurt people, hurt people!" Our words hold a lot of weight and each one of the words that we speak has the power to change our world. Those that are close to us always have the opportunity to hurt us more than those that we don't care about. We have to set realistic expectations with people so we can at least decrease the amount of potential hurt we will experience. In addition, setting boundaries is very important for everyone in our lives. Frustration and negative words quickly have more of a chance to come out when we do not set clear boundaries. The boundaries let them know there are certain lines they cannot cross. The boundaries keep you safe from the dangers that accompany uncomfortable situations. Managing your mouth gives you the courage and confidence to set realistic boundaries with everyone in your life.

Speak up!

When you meet someone for the first time there is nothing wrong with explaining your expectations -- don't feel that you are being arrogant and prideful -- you are being cautious and realistic. If you are honest with a potential mate or a person that you are thinking about dating, this can only help the relationship. When you are not managing your mouth in the area of relationships you can find yourself disappointed and in the midst of the memory of another relationship gone bad. At the same time, you have to be careful who you allow close to you because there are some men/women that will not value you with the words that they speak. Since words are very powerful, we cannot assume that we can handle the agony and stress that is attached to some people's words. Communication is a major problem in a lot of relationships, but because it takes so much work, most people would rather quit. If a relationship means something to you, it will take effort from both parties. Put this book down and write down some areas where you know that you can improve in the area of communication. After you identify these areas you need to work on, take immediate action and start working on these areas.

Since you are the one reading this book, you are taking the first step to changing the way you communicate with your potential mate. If you put the right amount of work into it, you will see how things will change. You don't have to give you opinion about every single thing. You don't have to fight back with words every time you feel offended. Sometimes it's best to sit and think about the best way to handle the situation. Unfortunately in relationships, some people will only allow you to meet their representatives by the words that they speak. They tell you what they believe you would like to hear, and most of it unfortunately is not the truth regarding who they really are. It's easy for a man or woman to say all the right things to get you on a date, to spend quality time with you, or to eventually form a relationship. It's a brand new story to be extremely honest about your situation and who you are at your core.

Place yourself around those that will speak life into in times that you might not be able to speak life into yourself. Get around people that are willing to encourage you, pray for you, and tell you how great you are when you might not feel so great. At the same time, place yourself around people that are willing to tell you the truth even at the risk of hurting your feelings. A true friend will be brutally honest with you and at the same time be your biggest cheerleader. Stop sharing your best with people that want to see your worst. The individuals that should be around you are those that are managing their mouths as well.

If someone is willing to disrespect the God-given gifts and talents that lie inside of you, then they don't deserve to be around you when those gifts and talents become manifested to the world. If someone is willing to speak death into you and discourage any chance they get, remove those individuals out of your life as soon as possible. Your road to success is already difficult enough, you don't need anyone riding along with you that will tell you how unsuccessful you will be, how much of a failure you are, or how much they don't believe in you. Unfortunately, some people are not that obvious, they will appear to be on your team, all the while practicing with your opponent. We can say that words don't hurt us, but if you have someone that claims to love and believe in you but speaks against you, that hurts more than a punch in the face.

Take action

You owe it to yourself to take action when you think of how much you have already been through. If it meant enough to you to speak it, it should mean enough to you to do it. I remember a very old television commercial where an older gentleman screamed. "Don't just stand there; do something!" This hit home to me even when I was a little boy; it taught me that being unproductive wasn't acceptable in our society. I feel the exact same way right now, I have to be productive and inactivity disturbs me. You might struggle with inactivity and/or being unproductive, but it all starts with your mouth. You have the ability to change things around right at this very moment with the words that come out of your mouth. There will be times when you might not feel like working towards your goals, but you have to keep pushing since you have become aware of how much potential lies inside of you.

So many times we have an epiphany or a clear realization of what we need to do but we never take action. Another area of managing our mouths that we need to consider is inaction. Would you agree that we talk a lot about what we're going to do, but never do it? Are you the guy or gal that speaks a lot about your dreams and goals but nobody ever sees any action out of you? Are you living an unproductive life based on the words you say? You have to hold yourself more accountable and make your words match up with your deeds. It makes no sense to spread all of your plans on the table to simply stare into a future that will never come true.

Be who you say you are. If you won't do it in public, don't do it in private. Instead of bragging about how great you are, let others brag for you based on the life they see you living. Be consistent with your lifestyle and the words that you speak. Be yourself. One of the greatest blessings that you can ever give to anyone is your true self. Nobody likes hearing from an inconsistent person; they might believe your false identity in the beginning but eventually they won't believe a word you have to say. If you know that you don't swear and you live by integrity, don't start swearing and acting immoral just to please the crowd! You are much better than that. If you know that you are faithful to your wife then don't even entertain conversations with the guys about the women at work, the gym, or at your local church; be who you say you are. The words that come out of your mouth should match up with your actions. This doesn't mean that you will be perfect, we all make mistakes from time to time, but when your goal is to remain consistent, you have to make the right choices.

Are you excited about your life? Without answering that question those around you already know by the words that you speak. Have you ever met someone that was chipper all the time and seemed like nothing in this world could ever ruin their day? I am not that person, and I'm sure that some of my readers don't fit into that category either. We all go through challenges in our lives that sometimes weigh us down; and it's easy to get discouraged. I have my days when I can be extremely hopeful about life, cheerful, and in an excellent mood; but other days I really have to press. During these tough days what kind of words are you speaking to yourself? The truth of the matter is we spend more time by ourselves than any other person in this world. Even if you constantly have other people around you, your personal thoughts inside your head dominate most of your decision-making. Even if you received an idea from someone else, you made a choice to continue entertaining that particular thought. Since we spend so much time with ourselves we have to make sure that we are speaking positivity instead of negativity.

There are enough negative things to focus on in this world through television, the radio, various conversations with people, or scrolling through social media. In the midst of difficult times the words we say to ourselves will either confirm how bad things really are, or persuade us to adopt a different perspective on our situation. Your thoughts truly run your life.

The same is true if things are going well for you; continue to reaffirm the fact that you are loved by God and He is getting things in store for you. The sad part about our society is that we focus too much attention on our weak areas and never seek to strengthen the areas that we are great in. We should definitely spend some time and attention on our weak areas, but if you never focus on your strengths then in some areas we will never reach our goals. For example, one of my gifts is encouraging people, and one of my weak areas is impatience with myself.

One thing that I have dedicated myself to is consistent self-improvement while allowing myself to enjoy special moments and not feel rushed to go towards the next goal. In order to do this I read a variety of different books, I watch documentaries on individuals that have overcome various difficulties, and take the time to evaluate how my weeks and months were to capture any improvement. I also research ways to help my clients within my life coaching program, receive feedback from close friends and family, and meet with my life coach on a weekly basis. At times it becomes challenging to work on my strengths and weaknesses in the midst of working on my goals because it can be a bit of a distraction; but I have to keep pressing. I also examine the words that I'm speaking to myself; and if they need to change; I change them.

When I look back and see the benefits of working on these areas of my life I end up gaining reassurance that I am doing the right thing. When we make the decision to work on improving ourselves we have to keep ourselves motivated with our words. When we get to that point of exhaustion our words will either remind us that it's not worth it, or we have to keep going. Too many times we look at ourselves in the mirror and are not pleased by what we see. We are able to tell ourselves that there is more that we can be doing, but when we think of the amount of work that it will take to get there, and end up retreating from our goals.

Watch what you say

I can't express enough about the importance of speaking life and not death to yourself. At times we might not have enough people around us to encourage us and tell us how great we are, so you have to tell yourself. If you get a place where you encourage yourself and strongly depend on what God has already said about you; you will no longer be swayed by someone else's negative opinions. Words can still hurt, but their words or negative opinions will no longer have the same effect on you as they use to. The main reason why their words hurt so much is because you have allowed them to enter a part of your heart that you are extremely vulnerable in. Being vulnerable is not a bad thing, it just means that you allow people the chance to love our hurt you. Instead of allowing your heart to become callus we have to allow ourselves to love and be loved. You can definitely keep yourself from being hurt by eliminating friends and never meeting anyone new, but that will also remove any opportunities for you to experience the joys and happiness of love. Some people will hurt us but we will also hurt other people from time to time.

One thing to be careful of are the words that come out of your mouth in relation to others. In the midst of certain arguments we can easily say things that we later regret, but unfortunately we can never take those words back. The way that we sometimes feel about people is bad and those feelings we have need be addressed. We don't always have to share with the other person that they hurt us or made us made. What we have to understand is, our hurt feelings are our hurt feelings, and even if we expressed how we felt that, doesn't guarantee the other person will experience the same intensity of feelings as we do.

When we get to that place of forgiveness with someone it's not about them, it's all about us. We can be free from un-forgiveness, hurt, and anxiety attached to the pain someone else caused. We don't need to retaliate with our words. Too many times we desire for someone else to experience hurt and pain because they inflicted that upon us. We have to walk in our individual freedom even if they are not involved. Keep in mind we can speak to others about our feelings and at times you will know if someone is going to be receptive enough to hear what you have to say. There will be other instances where you will know that this is the wrong time to talk, or that you shouldn't talk at all.

You also have to be careful saying negative things about someone simply because you are having a tough time with them. This is very important in marital relationships. You might be extremely close to a parent, sibling, or have a best friend that you share a lot of personal details with about your marital struggles. The problem with this is while you and your spouse eventually make up from the disagreement, the other person continues to build their own perception of this person based on the stories you have shared with them. It's not that you shouldn't share your feelings and have the opportunity to vent, but you have to be careful making your spouse seem like such a horrible person. In addition, the same is true for other relationships especially at work. When a co-worker or manager is not exhibiting the right behavior whether it be unethical or simply not to your personal liking; sometimes it's best to keep your mouth closed. At times co-workers are not as trusting as we would like them to be; and some of the venting and sharing of feelings regarding of other employees and management can quickly turn to your disadvantage.

I experienced the damaging of effects of not managing my own mouth at work. I was hired on as a new manager and given as a first task to rally the department together to identify areas where they wanted to see the department improve. I listened intently for a couple of weeks while I allowed each staff member to vent with pure confidentiality. With all the information I gathered and brought back to the department head, there were definitely going to be some changes made that would in turn bring more productivity and effectiveness to the entire organization.

Now here is where the story makes a turn for the worse. During my one-on-one sessions with a few of the staff members I shared with them my thoughts of a few of the staff members, which they shared with my director. Being that I was a new employee to the company, and still needed to prove myself, it was important to act with integrity as a good leader with my staff. I should have acted more responsibly and with more wisdom. This was definitely a bad idea and within the next week I lost my job. The reason my director fired me was because I acted inappropriately as a manager and I threw off team cohesion. That was definitely a lesson learned for me to keep my mouth shut, and learn to use more wisdom in the words that I spoke. Who's managing your mouth?

Chapter 7-Who's managing your emotions?

This is an area that I struggled in for a long time. Being able to manage my emotions was not only hard but also extremely stressful. Allowing other people to make me mad, make me feel insecure, make me uncomfortable in certain settings, make me anxious, make me doubtful, make me afraid, and make me nervous were just a few of the emotional roller coasters I found myself in. A roller coaster's job is to go extremely fast, have many loops and turns, provide a thrill, excitement, and a bit of fear. Does that sound like some of the emotions you have experienced? The tough part about emotions is that people cannot initially see how you feel on the inside until that emotion takes physical form after you have lost control over them.

Are you in control?

As I mentioned before in a previous chapter, I experienced a series of failed relationships in which the mismanagement of my emotions was easily seen. I found myself with a chip on my shoulder and lacked the ability to control my feelings. I would often make rude comments to the person that I was dating at the time due to some type of hurt that I felt during that occasion. Often times, we retaliate and go into defense mode when we feel we are being attacked or done wrong by someone else. I would also tend to say smart comments that rubbed those of whom I was in a relationship with the wrong way. My emotions were all over the place from past hurt that was never properly dealt with. The truth of the matter is, I struggled with thoughts of rejection, fear, and abandonment. Even though there were some great people in my life during that time, because of past pain, the majority of them were pushed away unconsciously. It's interesting that we can say out of our mouths that we desire successful relationships that will eventually turn into marriage, but we destroy and dismantle them by our lack of understanding of how to manage our own emotions.

It wasn't anyone else's responsibility to manage my emotions for me; this was my job in which I had no training for. Going through a period of blaming everyone else for leaving me, hurting me, and not knowing how to treat me, I got nowhere in my discovery of how to manage my own emotions. Through these experiences I became a "people-pleaser" who jumped at the opportunity for someone to accept me for me, or at least for the person that I was appearing to be. I cannot tell you how many times I changed my perception, plans, and feelings based on someone else's opinion. This brought me into a very weird place where I had no idea who I really was and what I wanted out of life and relationships. I can remember when I was engaged to be married to an awesome young lady that I met at my church. The relationship was going really great and we had our wedding date finalized with all the particulars handled. Someone that I had respected a lot advised against the marriage based on how they felt. They explained that I could do better and they weren't totally convinced that I truly loved this young lady or not. I had very strong feelings for this woman and was in love, in spite of how they interpreted my feelings. Unfortunately, because I was so wrapped up in pleasing this individual I spoke to my fiancé and called the wedding off.

To this day I often wonder what kind of marriage her and I could have had if I had control over my emotions. This hurt eventually caused her to leave our local church; walking away with the horrid memories of a man with a mismanaged lifestyle. We find ourselves in a dangerous place when we not only take advice from people, but we totally dismiss what we know to be true for a mirage of external truth. A mirage in and of itself appears to be real, but the closer that you get to it you find out the truth. Think back to the classic cartoons where the character is in the desert and desperately thirsty for a drink of water and magically a mirage of water appears. The character soon runs quickly to the mirage, but is sorely disappointed when he finds out it was not reality. The same was true for me plenty of times when I put my trust in someone else's opinion, which guided my emotions in distorted ways. Without trying to determine what was right for me I continued in my "people-pleasing" cycle, which gave my managers more control over my emotions.

Passion

Another part of managing your emotions that I would like to discuss is your passion. The word is so powerful and often used is destructive ways. There is a side of passion that I want to discuss regarding goals and ambition. One definition describes it as the powerful, compelling emotion or feeling as love or hate. Another definition brings to light exactly the type of passion that I will be referring to; a strong fondness, enthusiasm, or desire for anything. In terms of reaching your goals, you need to develop at stronger desire and passion for them. No longer can you sit back with a small desire to achieve great success.

Some of the greats in our era such as Steve Jobs, Oprah Winfrey, Larry Page and Sergey Brin of Google, all developed this sickening work ethic and most important passion for their dreams and goals. That same passion is needed for us to be great and even more to be phenomenal. Eric Thomas once said "be phenomenal or we can be forgotten." That passion will keep you when you want to give up. That passion will remind you why you are doing it in the first place. And let me stop there and say if your dream is to be rich and not help change the world then you need to get a new dream. Your dream should never collide with your God-given purpose to help change the world for the better. Now our passion creates the momentum, focus, drive, dedication, persistence, and tenacity that we all need when times get hard. It's really hard to explain if you've never had a passion for anything. I'm not talking about a romantic passion that could go away if you're not getting along with the person or are no longer attracted to them romantically. The passion that I'm speaking about it keeps you up at night, and wakes you up early in the morning to get closer to achieve the goals that are attached to it.

This passion is similar to the excitement you feel when you know a gift will be arriving soon that you having been expecting. It's comparable to being pregnant in that you feel the baby inside you moving and there are definitely signs that there is another life in you but the world cannot see it yet. This passion is so uniquely tied to your emotions that managing this passion is going to take a lot of responsibility on your part. Unfortunately, no matter how much you want to share your passion with certain people you will have to keep your mouth closed. You won't be able to share all of your ideas, goals, and plans with certain people because they are not ready to see your baby.

If anyone has ever been to the hospital when a child is being born you can identify with the fact that the doctors and nurses only allow a select few to come into the hospital room. They don't do this to be mean or inconsiderate; they do this because there is a limited amount of space in the room and they want to decrease the amount of commotion the woman has to experience while giving birth. The doctors realize that she has to go through enough pain in the process of giving birth and any added stress or drama will make the process even more difficult. That is the same way your process is with birthing out the passion and dreams inside of you. Everybody can't be around you during certain seasons of your life. When you are finally giving birth you will have to kindly tell some people to wait in the lobby. Even after you have given birth and the world is ready to see your child you still only invite certain people to your home, and even fewer people to visit you in the hospital room. The main thing to understand is that your passion has to be cared for and nurtured as if it was your child. You cannot listen to negative people tell you that your idea won't work, too many people are doing it, you're not going to make it, it's too hard, just be patient.

Everyone will not understand why you are passionate about certain things, and more frustration will come when you try to explain it to unpassionate people. You have to surround yourself with those that have their own passion and will allow you to flow in yours. If your mind is not truly made up about that dream or goal then you haven't developed a passion for it yet. I'm not saying that you won't ever be doubtful, scared, or worried, but you have to make up in your mind that you are going after that dream by any means necessary. What some people don't understand is that their dreams are too big for some people, and that strong passion you have regarding your dream does not fit into their box.

It's okay to not be okay

Have you ever allowed yourself to be free to grieve, let out your pain, and be totally comfortable being vulnerable for a season? Sometimes we go through some really difficult times and feel as if we need to rush through the healing or grieving process. Let me encourage you, if you are still breathing that means that last storm you just came out of didn't kill you. That last painful relationship didn't make you lose your mind. You still have the ability to think, see, smell, breathe, and taste; and that is a reason to get excited. You don't even have to read someone else's story to find hope and courage to get through your pain; you can look back on all the things that God brought you out of and be reminded of how strong you really are.

What is interesting is that some of the things we thought we couldn't live without, we have lived without. Someone once told me that sometimes you have to go through pain to get out of pain. Just as forgiveness takes time and is a continual process in many instances, grieving works the same way. Allow yourself to be free to feel all the emotions attached to that hurt and pain that you experienced. We can try our best to put on a show and act as if there is no pain, but you can only be phony for so long. We might be able to fool the rest of the world, but looking at yourself in the mirror will always require the truth to come out. We can't run from our pain, nor can we ever escape, we have to deal with it. Some of the things you went through as a child definitely was not your fault; some of the experiences you had in your early twenties weren't your fault either. What you are responsible for is what you do with your pain. If you choose to retaliate because of the pain that was caused towards you or someone you loved, that is not managing your emotions correctly. I can only imagine how difficult it must be to live each day after the misery that person put you through, or the constant abuse you experience at the hands of them without anyone to rescue you; that is tough. All I am asking for you to do is to take at least 1% responsibility for how you react to what happened to you. I'm not asking you to take responsibility for the entire downfall of that relationship or the hurt that was caused, but only how you react to what happened to you.

Managing your emotions takes a brave person, since you have to take accountability for how you deal you're your emotions, whether good or bad. At the same time there is another area of managing our emotions that some people neglect. When you are extremely happy and/or excited about something you still have to manage your emotions because the excitement can push you to make decisions that you should not have made. Have you ever been in a romantic relationship with someone that is treating you just how you want to be treated, saying all the right things, and you end up saying, "I love you" too soon because your emotions were so high? Or have you been super-duper happy about a particular idea that you rushed into making plans that were premature? Our emotions can take us to places we might not be ready for. As a life coach and motivational speaker I push people to go after their dreams and goals, but being too caught up in our emotions can definitely hurt us.

Rollercoaster ride

I used to be extremely caught off guard by my emotions. Whenever I dated someone I would allow my emotions to get out of control very quickly. I wanted to take things slow, but my impatience usually got the best of me and I said and did things based on my emotions and not actual wisdom. Being managed by my emotions was a very dangerous thing; especially considering the fact that I honestly thought I was in control the entire time. The thought of having a successful romantic relationship made my heart take me where my mind wasn't ready to go. The strange part about relationships is that when you experience so many bad ones you have high hopes for the first thing that resembles what you know you deserve. It's not so much that you are impatient, but the reality is that being single can be lonely and annoying at times. We might enjoy rollercoaster rides at amusement parks, but not in real life.

Regardless of how you feel you have to be sure you guard your emotions. It's not that the person is not trustworthy with your heart but you have to protect yourself and them from you. Emotions can be healthy and can definitely help us steer clear of danger in terms of fear, anxiety, and stress, but it can also be used against us. If you know you are not ready to commit to an exclusive relationship with that man or woman, don't tell them how much you care about them and see yourself being with them for the rest of your life. Those words will make any normal human being get excited and want to consider the possibilities that you are entertaining. Just like if you tell someone that you hate them and never want to see them again; they will not want to continue phone or text conversations with you.

It's important to protect other people's emotions by the decisions we make with our words and actions. You never want to send someone on an emotional roller coaster just because you feel a certain way. Use wisdom and let those feelings settle in for a few days or even weeks to see if they are consistent. Many times we get on an emotional high about a relationship or a particular thing at the moment but shortly after you think everything through you often have to retract your statement and apologize for your actions. Late night conversations in dating relationships are really the worse time to be caught up emotionally. You are sunk into your coach or buried under your covers and pillows on your bed and you become the most romantic person in the world. A lot of things are said because your head is in the clouds; in a sense, it's almost like being intoxicated by drugs or alcohol. Our emotions are very powerful and they should never be taken lightly.

You might be currently going through a horrific marriage where your spouse doesn't value you, purposely disrespects you, pushes all of your buttons, doesn't provide the love you need, and makes it a point to remind you of how rough your life would be without them. You feel like he/she is stabbing you over and over again with a weapon that will not penetrate far enough to kill you, but painful enough to make you feel like you're already dead. It's unfortunate that you have to go through this, but you can survive you through it. If you take a few minutes to look back over your life there have been some amazing things that you bounced back from. No matter how tragic these times are for you right now, I ask and even beg you to keep pushing. Seek some counseling, communicate your feelings to him/her, speak to a Pastor, but please give it another shot. If you have tried all these things then take some time to pray for guidance, and evaluate if you need to separate from the marriage, or call it quits all together. Above all else, don't simply give up because times are hard right now; you can get through this like everything else you have gotten through.

This might in fact be the most difficult time in our life, but you can make it through this. If nobody around you believes in you, I dare you to start believing in yourself. You are more amazing than you realize. I'm not saying that this pain doesn't hurt day in and day out, but every single day God is providing you with more strength to face another day. Gaining strength through these difficult times might not have been your ultimate goal, but this is your reality. Being strong doesn't mean that you don't cry and deal with your pain, being strong is recognizing what you can and cannot do in this situation, and having the courage to handle your responsibilities.

It hurts because you do really care

One of the main reasons it hurts so bad is because you really did care about that person. If they were just another person you were dating and having fun with it wouldn't really matter to you; but the fact that you put your heart out there and it got crushed, that's why it hurts so bad. You had high expectations that this would be the last time you would be dating someone, and this relationship would lead to marriage. We care about people so much that we put our hearts out there to be hurt, at the risk of being truly loved. Learning to forgive can be a challenge but it is definitely something that is needed for a single man or woman in the world of dating. We all have to use more wisdom in the area of dating because in some instances we know that some people are not right for us, but we entertain the idea anyway.

You are not in high school anymore and for some this is not your first year in college for you to experience what works and what doesn't. Take the time to identify what you can and cannot put up with regarding relationships and don't compromise. Your heart, mind, and emotions are too valuable to be played with by people that mean you no good. Only those that desire to truly experience love will also have an opportunity to truly experience hurt. There are those that grow bitter, cold, and resentful from failed relationships; not realizing that there are lessons to be learned from every interaction and relationship we have with someone. It might have hurt, but realize that you are human, you have a heart, and you actually cared about that person.

Take control of the wheel

Are you tired of your feelings running rampant? Do you want to take back the control over your emotions? Have you reached the point where you can no longer deal with someone else in charge? Managing your emotions can take a lot of effort but it is worth your time and energy. With the amount of frustration that some of us have experienced associated with other people I believe that walking away from old management styles and adopting new ones will allow us to experience the freedom we all desire.

Declare today will be the last day that another person will control your life or your emotions. Nobody in this world has that much power over you that they determine how you feel and what behaviors you exhibit. You are in control of your own emotions, and regardless of an argument, disagreement, or mistreatment; you determine your reaction. Knowing how to experience various feelings without acting out those feelings is a sign of maturity. There will be times when we experience hurt and feelings of anger, madness, confusion, or become furious, but managing our emotions means that you take the time to figure out your next move and what will be best. Unfortunately, if you take a trip down memory lane you will see how many occasions you have not managed your emotions correctly, and how that reaction has dramatically affected your life in some type of way. What we all need to realize is that we set in motion various things by the decisions that we make.

Many of us get frustrated at our jobs and often lose control; blurting out comments and insults about our co-workers and bosses that put our livelihoods at stake. I can't imagine how stressful that job can be at times. The fact that you enter that company day in and day out giving your all and are never appreciated and extremely under-valued and under paid. That is enough to make you scream and walk out of there without even considering how your bills are going to get paid. You experience the agony of dealing with certain co-workers, their attitudes, and maybe even a boss that doesn't respect or value the service that you provide to the company. It also becomes difficult to perform the same duties over and over again when you know that nothing will change as far as obtaining a raise or promotion. It's overwhelming to think about being in a rate race in your career, with no other options available.

Most individuals experience this same frustration every single day. You have to manage your emotions at work as well, which becomes very difficult to do, trust me I know. If there are things about your job that you can change, change them, if you can't then consider finding a new job, going back to school, or working on a dream or goal that will eventually get you out of that job. Don't complain; be grateful that you have a job right now. There is nothing wrong with venting, but there is a thin line.

Let's look at this closer... A successful woman working towards becoming a partner at a law firm has a sister that just doesn't seem to know what she's doing with her life. The sister has had several failed relationships and is on the edge of yet another. This time is a little more challenging because this boyfriend has a drinking problem, and she is pregnant. The lawyer is also an upset manager that has an employee in her sister that doesn't seem to listen to her advice. No matter how many times the manager speaks to her employee she continues to go down the same road that has proven to be unsuccessful for her. She has explained to her sister over and over again that she needs time alone, don't date anyone for a year to get over the last boyfriend, and when guys ask for her number tell them she is not interested. Unfortunately, she never listens to this advice and every time a handsome guy with a good job comes along she falls for the bait. The sister is finally ready to listen to her manager's suggestions so she schedules a meeting with her. While over dinner at her manager's house the employee cries and cries over her current circumstances, actually apologizing to her manager for all the bad mistakes she had made over the years.

The manager begins to speak very firm and harsh explaining that she should have listened to her before, now she is alone again but this time with a child to take care of with only a part-time job. The lawyer now feels it is her sole responsibility to take care of her sister since she doesn't have anyone else to help. The employee (sister) has been given strict orders to contact her manager on a weekly basis of her progress and not to take advice from her parents, friends, or anyone else except for her. The employee has been told she is not a responsible person, she cannot reach her goals by herself, she will fail without her manager's help, and her manager is the only one that cares about her. The reason the sister is called the employee is because the manager for her life is her sister the lawyer.

There is a huge problem with someone thinking you can't make it without their help. Get up man, get up woman and take your life back from whoever is trying to run it without you. If you are someone that has experienced failure in your past, you are not alone because every human being in this world experiences failure at some point in their lives. Manage your emotions by removing the fear and regret that you feel and pressing ahead. The interesting thing about failure is that it makes you better and you have the chance to learn from it. If you only experience successful events in your life there is nothing to learn at all. Can you stop reading this book for a few minutes and tell yourself something? I want you to say this very slowly:

"I AM THE MANAGER OF MY OWN LIFE, AND IT DOESN'T MATTER HOW MANY MISTAKES I HAVE MADE, I AM IN CHARGE."

Making this declaration unlocks the door to a realization that your life is your responsibility. In the chapters ahead we will go a little bit deeper into certain areas of our lives. Stop giving others permission to run your life, welcome some suggestions, feedback when requested, and the criticism from others in order to grow as a man or woman, but never give full control over to anyone. God created us to be good stewards over our lives; and if you look at the word steward, it means manager.

Feelings of insecurity and an overall lack of self-confidence can become overwhelming and extremely exhausting. When these feelings arise, at times you cab inadvertently hurt yourself or someone else if you don't manage them quickly. Insecurity doesn't have to define you and it doesn't have to control your decision-making. When it springs up, it can rob you from meaningful friends, opportunities, and enjoyment that you deserve. Believing the lies of insecurity will make you unsure of your God-given abilities, strengths, and courage that you can make it through difficult times or achieve a particular task. Insecurity makes you look at yourself in the mirror and become unpleased with the way you look, dress, or perform in front of others.

One thing we all need to realize is we are not on stage 24 hours a day to make the crowd happy; if you feel contentment with who you are, that should be enough. There will always be people that are not happy with decisions that you make, an outfit that you put on, or the way that you look; that is there problem not yours. We have seen a multitude of individuals that are not happy with a particular body part or feature and they get cosmetic surgery done to improve or enhance the way that they look. In some cases the surgery is understandable and was needed; in other cases the surgery was merely to make this individual feel better about themselves.

A lack of self-confidence can play a toll on your emotions because you never honestly feel that you can compete with the rest of society. You oftentimes retreat into your proverbial corner, downtrodden with a look of defeat written all over your face. There is a man or woman that will love you just the way that you are; you are beautiful, smart, gifted, and amazing; remember that please! Little do you know that the challenges that you have experienced are not that rare for most people that have huge goals and are uncomfortable with being average. Your emotions need to be managed properly when your self-confidence is running low. Anger, fear, happiness, sadness, excitement, joy, and madness are all feelings, which are part of your emotions; it's okay to have them.

Although some of these feelings might come upon you unaware, you still have the ability to make a decision about what you will do with those feelings when they do arise. In addition, you don't have to apologize for your feelings, because they are your feelings; you only need to apologize for your reaction to your feelings if they make you come out of character. Some people will try to push you to make bad decisions because they like to reaffirm the fact that you have areas of improvement that need to be made. They like to show the world that you are not who you say you are and the remarkable things the world has seen from you is all a fallacy. During the time that I was a people pleaser I felt like I was performing on Broadway every time I walked out the door. I felt the crowd was always watching and I needed to give them my very best every show. You have to live your life for you and not for someone else; the emotional ups and downs attached to pleasing others will continue to limit you from achieving your best.

You are much better than some of the stuff that you put up with. You do not have to live in fear or torment from another human being; no matter who they are. Some people feel that they have power over you to control you, manipulate you, and make you live in so much fear that you cannot make any decisions without their approval. You are not some weak man or woman that needs someone else's permission to live and obtain your future goals. There is much more in you than you might realize. The struggles you have experienced in your past have not only made you stronger, but they have given you the courage to press even further than you originally though you could go. The emotional turmoil, aguish, and pain that you are currently putting up with needs to be evaluated. You do not have to go into another year the same way. Realize your worth!

Some people will be shocked and amazed when they finally see your strength and how you no longer need their permission to be great. It might seem like a roller coaster ride that you have been on these last few months due to the crazy relationship that you currently have with him/her. Please don't limit this emotional turmoil to a romantic partner only; this also applies to family relationships, work relationships, and close friendships. Get off that rollercoaster ride and leave the park; don't even worry about a refund. If you noticed, a larger part of this book has been dedicated to pushing you towards your destiny and achieving the goals you currently have sitting on the shelf. With that said, some people cannot remain in your life if you are going to get to your next level. Now it doesn't mean that they are bad people, they just might be bad for you; at least during this season. Learn what you can from the relationship and move forward. Some of these relationships you will be able to savage and set some realistic boundaries for. Others you will have to walk away completely in order to keep your sanity.

If you allow someone to continue treating you the same way, you will continue to feel confused, frustrated, and an emotional wreck. You cannot blame them if you choose to stay and put up with that emotional pain. Part of the confusion stems from you realizing you deserve more, but not wanting to give up on yet another relationship. There is nothing wrong with persistence, but sometimes you can be persistent for the wrong thing. Instead of having faith that they will do better, believe within yourself that you deserve better. The individuals that are loyal to you and have been dedicated to pushing you deserve your appreciation. You can begin to live a stress-free life if you remove people that are not helping your progress and place people in your life that will actually help you. At times we don't appreciate people enough that are actually there for us. We focus too much attention on those that are not there for us or making us feel undervalued. We all have to manage our emotions in every area of our lives.

Chapter 8-Who's managing your future?

I start this chapter with a story of Carl who doesn't have control of his own life and is being managed by someone else. Carl wakes up each day knowing that he is destined for more and feels he has a purpose that is different from the one that has been created for him. Being upset at his lack of overall productivity, he shouts, screams, and cries occasionally, as he looks at himself in the mirror. His job is so depressing and extremely stressful. He hates even the thought of waking up to an alarm clock that reminds him of the dreadful day that is waiting for him. Weekends are no better since the various household tasks he needs to complete nag and annoy him more than a dripping faucet. The problem is he is alone. Oh sure, Carl has plenty of friends, family, and those he holds casual conversations with at work, but he is still alone.

He calls his parents for advice on what he should do about his finances, relationships, spirituality, money issues, work problems, emotions, education, and his future. They give him advice based on their own past experiences and what they think would be best for him. Carl doesn't need any more opinions from his parents, friends, or co-workers. They cannot provide the best advice for him because they have no idea who Carl really is. The truth of the matter is Carl cannot tell them who he is either because he has never taken the time to truly understand what he wants in life. Carl is a 35-year-old man that has no dreams, no vision, and no goals. He never believed those things were important since most of the people around him never achieved the success they were reaching for.

The time is now

This part of the book is definitely one of the most important. I will spend a great deal of time in this chapter examining the importance of your future and why managing your future should be of utmost importance to you. With that in mind, what goals do you currently have that are not being pursued due to mismanagement? Who is currently stopping you from going after that seemingly impossible goal? When will you muster up enough courage to discard those negative opinions that others have of you? When did you stop dreaming? The commitment that you made to yourself needs to be kept, by any means necessary. Who told you that your dreams, goals, and plans were too ridiculous to achieve? That person(s) in charge of managing this area of your life should be fired immediately without severance package as they depart.

What you will find out if you haven't already is that a lot of people want to manage your future. For the family members and friends that never got a chance to live out their own dreams, many will ask you to participate in this endeavor to see their dreams unfold. You have the ability to manage your future and make the decisions that are geared towards your best interests and not theirs. Because of your past and the bad decisions you have made, you might feel as though your future has already been determined, which does not show any promising signs. You have a life ahead of you that nobody else is in charge of, except for you. You might be plagued with a large amount of stress, depression, anxiety, and even thoughts of suicide, but you can take control today and turn your life around.

Starting today you can rise above the depression and anxiety that you feel. No longer being tormented by your past mistakes you can take the proper steps that are needed to turn your life around. Your future should mean something to you. I want you to realize even right now that your life is not over and it does have meaning. What you might not understand is that we create our reality. If your reality is that you're broke and things will never be better than your past; those thoughts will seep into your future. If you believe you will never be good in relationships that will be your reality. If you create a reality where depression and stress are in control then you could possibly live the rest of your life never experiencing your best. If you create a reality where joy, peace, and happiness reside then you will see a life worth living. Have you ever noticed that when you are experiencing the goodness of life even your storms and troubles cease to affect you? It's not that these problems are not there, but you have tapped into an area of your life that says, "I'm in charge of how I interpret the problems in my life." With this basis, the tough areas of your life that you cannot change, you will gain a new perspective on how to deal with them.

You have a lot to accomplish and contrary to what you might believe you don't have a whole lot of time. It took me nearly ten years to write this book because I thought that I could take my time and there wasn't a need to rush. Rushing is one thing but moving like a snail is another. It also took me 12 years complete my Bachelor's degree. After finishing my Bachelor's degree I did gain some momentum and went right into my Master's degree program and completed that. As of the writing of this book I am two years away from completing my Doctorate of Education degree in Organizational Leadership. Part of the reason that it took me so long to get started on my future is due to fear. Deep down inside I knew that I was made for more and that I would be great one day but taking the initial steps to get there seemed so difficult. It didn't help that most of my friends and family weren't going after their dreams with any effort either, so I became comfortable and complacent. I looked at my future as if it were a million miles away and there was no way I was ever going to get to accomplish the huge goals I knew were inside of me. So I waited and waited until it became too annoying for me to ignore my purpose calling me. Most of us have heard or are at least familiar with the "Deepest fear..." quote by Marianne

Williamson from her book entitled: "A Return to Love," but I want to spend some time examining a deeper meaning of it.

"...Our deepest fear is not that we are inadequate. Our deepest fear is that we are powerful beyond measure. It is our light, not our darkness that most frightens us. We ask ourselves: Who am I to be brilliant, gorgeous, talented, and fabulous? Actually, who are you not to be? You are a child of God. You're playing small does not serve the world. There is nothing enlightened about shrinking so that other people won't feel insecure around you. We are all meant to shine, as children do. We were born to make manifest the glory of God that is within us. It's not just in some of us; it's in everyone. And as we let our own light shine, we unconsciously give other people permission to do the same.
As we are liberated from our own fear, our presence automatically liberates others."

As stated above we are not afraid because we are inadequate, we actually know and believe how powerful and great we really are, and that is the scary part. That is part of the reason why we get paralyze when it comes to our goals and dreams because of the fear of being so great. It sounds strange to say but it's overwhelming when God shows you a vision of how great He has made you to be and you're stuck between "getting started" and "success." I know first-hand how difficult it can be to realize your purpose but not see how you're going to get there. Realizing how great you are can be a scary experience; it's not arrogance, its confidence. There is a thin line between arrogance and pride, and knowing who you were called and made to be. Humility is definitely important as you continue to reach success and are provided more opportunities to change the world, but never lose your self-confidence and drive.

We were made to shine bright like a diamond, and sometimes that brightness will irritate others that have positioned themselves in darkness. As you are climbing towards your goals, you have to realize that you are no better than anyone else, you have just chosen to accept the greatness that's inside you. Everyone on this earth was made and shaped with a purpose inside of them, few actually accept the challenge because of the difficulty of the assignment they were given. You cannot continue to play it safe for the convenience of other people. They might not want to grow but that doesn't mean that you have to stop because they are uncomfortable with what they see. Playing it safe and not taking some kind of risk will never get you to where you want to be. Sometimes you are placed in a situation at the right place and at the right time; and that is your golden moment of opportunity. If you don't take advantage of that opportunity you might miss your chance. Sure, there will be other opportunities that come back around, but it will never be exactly the same since that special moment has passed. You are great, dope, awesome, brilliant, magnificent, terrific, wonderful, and amazing. We were made in the image of God and if He is all those things I mentioned, then allow yourself to be described that same way. Why can't you be amazing? Who told you that you weren't awesome? Why can't you be called brilliant; your past doesn't define you! Managing your future sometimes means removing those negative voices out of your life permanently because there is only room for positivity.

Bring something to the table

For the world to continue to change for the better it needs you to take your rightful place and play your position. You cannot get caught up with someone else's dreams, goals, and purpose. God gave you a particular assignment and that needs to be followed. You have not been equipped with the necessary components to be someone else. The longer that you wait to walk into purpose the longer you will feel frustrated, unfulfilled, and miserable. Those that find purpose find peace and contentment because they know they are exactly where they need to be. There are some that need to hear what comes out of your mouth either through speech, a book, a poem, or some other way of encouragement. Your future solely depends on you. I cannot force you to walk into your purpose and realize your worth; you have to find that within yourself. If you notice, those that are trying to be someone else never reach their goal of actually doing it. Since they have lost themselves in an effort to be them, they become nobody. Your purpose no matter how big or small it is, is your purpose. Don't get caught up in the lights and glamor; if your role is to be in the background then be in the background. You might be a number two in the form of an assistant, or vice president, or a backup to someone in charge; don't envy their position, play your position. There is nothing wrong with aspiring to walk into that number one spot, but in the meantime be the best number two in the world in that role.

Don't let anyone be better at being you than you. There might be people with more education, more training, more experience, that come from a privileged background, but make up in your mind that they will never be better than you at being you. It is difficult to believe that you will influence millions of lives by your words because you don't see any indication of that being true. You have to hold onto your faith during those times of disbelief and doubt, and in so doing you will give others that same courage to believe in themselves and achieve their dreams.

You cannot have the future you want by holding onto the past that you don't want. There has to be a distinct difference between where you were, and where you hope to be. All of us from time to time get caught up in our past; thinking of the "should've", "could've", and "would'ves." We cannot go back in time to change our past, but we can change our future so our eventual past doesn't become something we don't want to remember. People love to take pictures; and as you can see from social media sites like Facebook and Instagram these photos are captured at various times, locations, or situations. These photos act as a reminder of where the person was so they can reflect back on the photos later with a smile or some delight. Our past works the same way, but in an opposite fashion. We often take so many mental photos of the pain, drama, and agony of a situation or event that it becomes rather easy to reflect back on those awful occasions. When we look back at our past we often ask ourselves questions to identify what state of mind we were in during those times to provoke us to put up with so much mess for so long. We look back too long and instead of using those past situations to become better, we end up becoming worse, due to the stagnation and complacency we place ourselves in. If your past indicated that some changes needed to be made to experience a better future; then it's time to produce those changes.

It starts with you

Looking within ourselves can be a very difficult and challenging ordeal, but its benefits far outweigh the struggles attached to it. You cannot take the old you into your future. There is no room for old bad habits, continual mistakes, bad relationships, bad choices with money, or doubt and fear. You were made to flourish and to become that awesome man/woman you know you were called to be; it's going to take some sacrifices. If you are annoyed by your weight, make the proper changes today and start somewhere. You might not see the results you want in a day, a week, or a month; but making some type of progress will at least build up some momentum to keep pushing you beyond your original limits. In terms of eating healthy it is not easy, and I will be the first person to tell you how enjoyable food is; it is absolutely amazing.

One thing you have to consider during that temporary fulfillment of eating your favorite food is, if you want to be sit back and forfeit all the progress that you have just made. If you have struggles with weight then it's time to take action. You don't have to be conquered by food. You don't have to necessarily look like a supermodel or bodybuilder, but you do need to care enough about your body that you monitor what goes into it and how much. Aren't you tired of looking at yourself in the mirror and being depressed afterwards? Aren't you tired of feeling self-conscious about yourself and afraid to enjoy life because of your weight? The time is now to take the proper steps to change your future. Join a gym, purchase a smoothie machine, consume more vegetables, and if nothing else please start to consume more water. You are an amazing human being with purpose inside of you. Don't allow your weight to make you feel inadequate or insecure. Things will get better for you when you decide to change. Don't beat yourself up about this part of your life; you have so much value and the world needs your gifts and talents. Yes, in the past you have been out of control with your eating habits, but today you have made a decision to do better and your life will never be the same.

If you decided to change your spending habits and work on your credit, then make some changes today to get you where you need to ultimately be. The amount of money that you currently make might not be enough to take care of all of your bills each month, so how on earth do you have extra money to go out every weekend? How do you have extra money to purchase new clothes and shoes whenever you feel excited? There are some that live in some very unsuitable places and have told themselves that they will soon be moving into a nicer place. Unfortunately, because of continued bad decisions with money it never seems like the right time. We cannot wait on our situation to get better we have to get better for our situation. Once your mind is made up about your financial situation you will create a budget and figure out how bad or good your credit report is. We have to push hard to become better financially, because I'm pretty sure you have some great ideas and plans that will take your financial situation being changed. You can't spend your money on everything you want by impulse. In addition, the way that we are teaching our children that same behavior is frightening. Our kids grow up thinking that it is perfectly normal to be bad with money and they should somehow blame society or the government with not giving them a fair share of resources. There are some cultures that do an excellent job with setting up a great future for their families and are extremely responsible with money; there are other cultures that have a long history of being horrible with money and play the "blame game." You can realistically make a small amount of money and still have the chance to set yourself and your children up for success.

Keep dreaming

I asked you earlier a very important question: "When did you stop dreaming?" The answer to this question will reveal much more about yourself in terms of where you are going. Becoming stagnate is something we as a people fall into because of mismanagement. Your future needs you to be an active participate in it. Constantly asking someone else's advice on what they think is best for you or where they think you should go is not an effective tool to obtain the answers you are truly seeking. What is that dream that you let die? Think about that dream for a few minutes and ponder on how successful or fulfilling it would have made you at this point in your life. Were you supposed to go back to school but never got up the courage to schedule your courses? Were you supposed to apply for that position at another company but through doubt and fear you were stopped at your tracks? That business inside of you is not going to start itself. Did you dismiss your great ideas and plans and adopt the thoughts that it will never work? There might be a book that can only be read if you have the courage to write it.

Your creativity is so different than the person you see as your competition; your gift to the world will never be seen or experienced unless you begin to live it out. Let's face it, you were not made the same as your friend, family member, co-worker or the person sitting next to you at your local church. Instead of you focusing your attention on someone else's gifts and talents, figure out what unique thing you can bring to the world and do that. You might play sports, be an engineer, be a writer, be a musician, a business owner, or even a stay at home mom; whatever your gift and primary skill is; work within that gift and perfect it. Has stagnation crept upon you? It might be time for you to put this book down again. Write down some goals, print them out, tape them up on your bedroom walls so you can see them every single day, and be accountable to them. One thing I figured out a long time ago was that nobody is going to reach my goals for me, and the ultimate accountability partner will always be me.

The bottom line is, some of us need to stop being lazy; get yourself up, and go after your dreams. Stop making excuses and start making adjustments. You are too grown to be making the same excuses you made when you were younger. If you want your dreams to happen, you have to get up out the bed and work towards them. You might have to turn off your notifications for Instagram and Facebook for a while. You might have to miss some of your favorite shows for a while. You might have to limit the amount of partying that you're doing to figure out your goals and dreams. And once you have them figured out you then need to work on your plan for executing them properly. And after that, you have to work on the plan that you have put together step by step. You might need to get off the phone from your favorite people and begin having conversations with people you might not normally talk to.

Get around people that will motivate you, encourage you, push you, be real with you, and most of all, and support you without any ulterior motives. I first thought about writing this book roughly a year and a half ago. I procrastinated for a long time because I didn't feel like writing it to be honest. I felt lazy and unmotivated until I started seeing so many of my friends and family members walking in their purpose and living out their dreams. Even then it still took me some time to work up enough courage to start working on this book. What you have to understand is that this book is not just for you, but it is also for me. As I am speaking to you, I am speaking to myself and the goal-seekers just like me. We have the drive and passion we need to go after our dreams.

Are you feeling as if you have no purpose and no excitement towards any goal or aspiration? It might be time for you to evaluate what you are feeding yourself mentally. If you are glued to the television 24 hours a day you might be hindering your future and preventing any flow of ideas and purpose to come to your mind. I once watched a documentary about Henry Ford that explained how hard he worked to reach success and how he had to limit the amount of distractions around him in order to keep pressing towards success. Even when he was one of the richest entrepreneurs in the world he still kept the same discipline he had before all the millions.

This same principle of discipline applies to us when managing our future. Nobody can exhibit discipline for you; this is something you have to do on your own. Whatever industry you are a part of, work hard to be the best in that industry; with integrity and good character. You never have to step on someone else's toes to reach success. If you stay in your own lane, what is meant for you will eventually come; there is plenty of success to go around. We sometimes get caught up trying to compare our gifts and skills to others; admiring their gift from afar and eventually becoming envious with the thought that their gift is better than ours. Your God-given gift is not the same as any other person on this earth; there might be some similarities, but there are some distinct differences. If you do research on all the individuals from various industries that are considered great they all have brought something special and a bit different to the world. Your idea and dream will help someone else's life become easier or at least less hectic. Someone's breakthrough is inside of the plans you refuse to make, the dreams you refuse to seek after, the drive you are too afraid to run with.

As you can see, managing our futures has a lot to do with our gift that we will present to the world. Living out your dreams and aspirations will ultimately provide peace and contentment, and the by-product of this will often times be financial security. Seeking after success merely for financial gain should never be our top priority; living in our purpose should be. When we are living in our purpose on purpose, it allows us to experience some of the same peace and serenity that you see on the faces of those you admire on television and in magazine articles. These individuals seem to have it all figured out in some aspects, or at least they appear that way. What most great people have figured out is that reaching success is only one part of it, maintaining that success takes just as much hard work and dedication as they had before they were well known.

It's worth the fight

Enjoying your life can give others permission to be free to enjoy their own. Being locked in a cage is no life for the bird with healthy wings. You are an extraordinary person with gifts, talents, and an explosive drive that can benefit the world. Are you tired of living in someone else's box? The city and state you live in, though it might be a great place, is not all there is to this world; there is so much more. There are people, places, and things you have not experienced, and I would argue that part of you longs to experience that. The passion that lies inside of you cannot stay hidden. There will never be a perfect time for you to start working on your dream. There will always be obstacles, set-backs, and circumstances that tell you that you cannot make it, and right now is not the time. I have talked myself out of many plans and goals because of insecurities, past failures, and disbelief. I had to get to a point where my belief system was stronger than my doubt system. Managing your own future is saying if I don't have anybody's assistance with my future, I will get out there and do it myself! You might have to give up some of your precious beauty sleep to say yes to your life, yes to your future, and yes to your goals.

Doing the difficult things to reach success is what makes the champions different from those that just play the game. The true greats in any sport from basketball, hockey, football, soccer, to baseball make up their minds early how hard they are willing to work to achieve their dreams. They have figured out that managing their own future has to be on the forefront of their minds if they're ever going to reach to top of their game. I don't believe that you're an average person, so please do me a favor and stop acting that way. If your life could be more consistent with what comes out of your mouth you will see dramatic changes in your relationships, your finances, and your future goals. Some of the issues that we run into is that we are not who we proclaim to the world that we are. Some would define this as hypocrisy, being fake or being phony; I would agree with them all and also add a lack of identity. Knowing who you really are keeps you away from some things that go against your values, beliefs, and character. If you don't know what you stand for it becomes very easy to fall victim to anything.

Les Brown once said, "The wealthiest place on the planet is the graveyard." He explains that in the graveyard there are hopes, dreams, aspirations that were never acted upon. There are ideas and inventions that were never realized. You don't want that said about you, do you? Some people are bold enough to create a bucket list, but others are bold enough to complete a bucket list. I don't believe you want to stay where you are because you realize there is something more inside of you. If you planned on finishing a goal this year and you haven't done it yet, get started today to finish it. Throughout this book we have discussed the matter of taking back control of your life in every area. Your future is going to be great if you allow it to be. You cannot live the same way any longer; something has to change.

Get started today

You have so much to live for and it doesn't matter how hard you have had it in the past; start living today. You are solely responsible for how your future turns out. If you look up three years from now and you are no further ahead, you cannot blame anyone else but yourself. There are some people that have an extremely hard life right now; you might be in a prison and you have more years left on your sentence then you want to remember; but be encouraged; you have a future too. Your decisions that got you to this place, do not define who you are. You might be housed in a homeless shelter or group home because of your past financial decisions or hardships, but you can get back up to.

Thank God for a place to rest your head but look around that place right now and say, "I won't be here for much longer." Our destinies have nothing to do with our past. Yes, in some ways our past decisions have shaped where we are right now, but make no mistake about it, your past and future are two different realities. You choose which one you want to live in. We can definitely learn from our past; there are areas in which we can make better decisions for our futures. Learning from our past also helps us to understand what we want and do not want in our future. It helps us identify who should stay and who should leave based on their past performances.

Managing your future is vitally important if you will reach the success that you yearn for. Don't allow someone else to tell you what you should be or should not be; that dream or goal that lies inside of you can be achieved no matter who is standing in the way. Don't just sit there and watch others be great, make them want to pull up a chair and admire your greatness as well. Many of us are living in the shadow of our parents' dreams and aspirations. They desire for you to achieve certain things so they can feel as if they actually did it through you. There are others as well that do the same thing.

Sometimes the people close to you will push you towards a goal, not necessarily because they want to see you succeed, but because they don't have enough confidence within themselves to go after it. They are seeing if an idea will work through your life. These individuals do not have the same courage, tenacity, and resilience as you; seeing you accomplish goals gives them the courage to do the same. Now in some aspects this can be a positive thing to encourage someone else; not so if these individuals are forcing you to dream their dreams and bring them into fruition. You have your own dreams to dream, goals to accomplish, and aspirations to go after, and you don't have time to confuse your purpose with ones that are being placed upon you.

Getting to where you need to be is not the responsibility of someone else; if no one else is willing to support you, then

YOU support YOU. The reality is there are times in our lives where we desire to be affirmed, appreciated, and supported, but when we don't; how will we react? We can choose to be bitter and resentful towards certain people, or we can realize that no matter how much we want them to it is not their assignment to support us. I strongly believe that God will send the right people that will support us; but keep in mind that everyone that supports us might not support every area of our lives. There are some that have been trained and equipped to only support certain areas and when they try to support other areas their work almost seems to be irrelevant. The problem is not that they are not trying; they just are not equipped. There are other individuals that genuinely want to help you and they do, but after a while their jealously and envy towards you begins to outweigh the support. In these times you can still get the support from them, but just understand that you might not want them too close to you. Managing our futures cannot be done by anyone else except you.

Conclusion

The overall success of your life is not dependent upon how much money you accumulate or the amount of gadgets, cars, and houses you own. True success is reaching a place of contentment within yourself and with what you have without taking advantage of someone else to get there. After reading each chapter you should by now have a brief understanding of why you make certain decisions whether they are harmful or helpful. Rediscovering who we are is vital towards reaching our goals and walking in continual purpose. We all have to let go of past hurts and the pain that is attached to them. You cannot go back and change the past but you can at least impact your future. Walking away with the understanding that you are brilliant even with your flaws and that you are remarkable with or without someone confirming it, is what I hope you were able to gather.

My reason for writing this book was to help change the entire world one heart, mind, and body at a time. It is important for me that you continue to press forward in realizing more of your own unique identity apart from the opinions of others. At this point in your life you have to say "by any means necessary." By any means necessary you will get out of debt, by any means necessary you will lose weight, by any means necessary you will have better relationships, by any means necessary you will be a better father or mother. There is no such thing as procrastination; most people have a priority problem.

As we go forward we cannot live in the regret from our past, nor are we forced to live in a miserable future. There is a reason you have been given purpose and goals to achieve. If you look back on all that you have survived you will realize that it wasn't luck or some special superpower that you had, but it was God keeping you for a reason. You are a world changer, and your unique gift will be used to influence, impact, and empower people all across this earth. Nobody can tell you that you haven't gained strength through those tough times; the average person would have lost their mind going through what you went through. There is nothing average about you, you go hard in every area of your life. Even when you look back on past experiences you are shocked to believe you made it through the fire as it were, without any burn marks. Your ability to bounce back from difficulty is a blessing to be appreciated and admired. There are some that go through a tough situation and they never recover from it. But not you, you are able to look at that situation in the face and know with assurance that things will get better.

You have been built for so much more than the temporary pain that you are dealing with currently. Regardless of how vulnerable and uncomfortable you feel right now, believe that you can make it through this. All of these storms you are experiencing has never caught God by surprise; He knows exactly how much you can take. Make up in your mind that you will not be defeated by this storm and you will rise above. Whoever you need to forgive, forgive them. You're not holding them back by not forgiving them; you're holding yourself back. It doesn't matter how terrible your past has been, that is not an indication of how your future will be. Your value in not dependent upon someone else's opinion of you, but ultimately how you see yourself. There is a remarkable person inside of you, waiting to obtain the permission to come out and show how great they really are. No longer can you play the background position and give everyone else the chance to be great instead of you. This is your time.

Keep in mind as you are on this journey of rediscovering yourself that you don't have to compete with anyone else. Take a look back at your own life and find areas that you can improve upon and let that be enough. Don't get caught up with the success or failure of another person; focus on yourself. At times we can spend too much time investigating someone else's steps to success that we pay no attention to how far we have come personally and how far we still need to go. There is nothing wrong with finding motivation and encouragement from other people, but when you see them as your competition that becomes a problem. In some respects competition might appear to be healthy, but the problem with competing with other people is that you spend too much energy dissecting every area of their lives. It would be better to focus on yourself and see how you can become better based on the goals you have set and what it will take for you to accomplish them. In addition, don't ever look at someone's failure and automatically write them off; you have no idea what they are doing behind closed doors. Yes they might have failed publically but that is not to say that can't eventually be right back on top or at least the position they fail from. We all need to have enough respect for others that we never rejoice when someone falls because we feel we now have an edge on them. If you need someone else to fail for you to be successful, your success is not built upon a solid foundation. There are enough of God's blessings to go around that we can celebrate others even if it's not the exact same lane that you are in.

You are more dynamic than you realize and the place that you're in right now is shaping you into the person that you ultimately need to become. As we come to the end of this book, I want to assure that you know within yourself that managing your life is hard to do, but it is so necessary. Stop devaluing who you are to make other people feel more comfortable. You won't be able to make everyone happy, but if you can put a smile on your own face sometimes that's more than enough. You have purpose inside of you and you cannot be caught up with who is not for you. There are some people in your life that truly matter and care for you, so focus on them.

Make sure they know how much you appreciate them and never take them for granted. Never stop asking yourself the all-important question: who's managing your life?

We had more faith in our dreams as kids; probably because

we actually believed they could come true.

~Manny Hall

For additional resources contact us at www.mannyhall.com

For booking Manny Hall for speaking engagements and/or for Manny Hall Life Coaching services contact us at www.mannyhall.com

This is a great resource for organizations trying to take their staff members to another level; churches to help their leadership staff to identify and walk in their purpose, and other small groups to discuss who is managing their lives.

Bulk book pricing is available for workshops, events, conferences, small groups, companies, ministries, and churches. Contact us for more information.

Made in the USA
San Bernardino, CA
10 January 2015